Over
It

Over It

Letting God Get You Past Life's Hurts

HAYLEY & MICHAEL DiMARCO

Revell
a division of Baker Publishing Group
Grand Rapids, Michigan

Hungry Planet

Published by Revell
a division of Baker Publishing Group
P.O. Box 6287, Grand Rapids, MI 49516-6287
www.revellbooks.com

Printed in the United States of America

Library of Congress Cataloging-in-Publication Data
DiMarco, Hayley.
Over it : letting God get you past life's hurts / Hayley and Michael DiMarco.
p. cm.
Includes bibliographical references.
ISBN 978-0-8007-3153-3 (pbk.)
1. Attitude change—Religious aspects—Christianity. 2. Suffering—Religious aspects—Christianity. I. DiMarco, Michael. II. Title.
BV4597.2.D56 2011
248.8′6—dc22 2011005055

Published in association with Yates & Yates, LLP, Literary Agents, Orange, California.

11 12 13 14 15 16 17 7 6 5 4 3 2 1

In keeping with biblical principles of creation stewardship, Baker Publishing Group advocates the responsible use of our natural resources. As a member of the Green Press Initiative, our company uses recycled paper when possible. The text paper of this book is composed in part of post-consumer waste.

green press INITIATIVE

CONTENTS

Chapter 1

GET READY TO

GET OVER IT

"Our yesterdays present ***irreparable*** things to us; it is true that we have lost opportunities which will never return, but God can **TRANSFORM** this destructive ***anxiety*** into a constructive thoughtfulness for the future. Let the past sleep, but let it sleep on the bosom of Christ. Leave the Irreparable Past in His hands, and step out into the ***Irresistible Future*** with Him."

Oswald Chambers, *My Utmost for His Highest*

Why Get Over It?

The past. Do those two words sound good or horrible to you? Your past might be something you miss, or it might haunt you. It might be a distant memory or a recurring nightmare. But whatever happened yesterday, the day before, or the year before, the past is part of your story. It's the path your life has taken to get you to where you are today and to make you who you are now. But no matter who you are, you probably have a few things in your past that you wish weren't there. Or you might have a ton. Whatever the case, the most important thing you need to know about your past mistakes, heartaches, pains, abuse, suffering, and misery is how to get over it.

Over It is our attempt to help you do that. We know that the things that have happened to you have impacted you. We know that they have made you who you are and that sometimes you don't like that fact and you want a change. We also know that the past can remain the present if you don't let go of it and get over it today (or maybe next week). And we know that guilt, resentment, bitterness, self-hatred, and fear can become a part of your normal, everyday life if you have a past that you haven't gotten over.

The average person has a lot of things that need getting over—things like guilt and pain from heartache, abuse, failure, weakness, bad memories, and loss. A sense that you can't forgive whoever or whatever it was that hurt you, even if it was yourself, can haunt you every day of your life that you fail to get over the past and to get on with today. And depending on what happened, the past can be more present than the present. Research has revealed that the cycle of grief can take significantly more time to get through when the loss is great. It takes you longer to get over the breakup of a relationship of two years than a relationship of two weeks, right? Well, not always. We've seen people who went out on one date with a person suffer from heartache for months after never hearing from them again. So no matter what the world says your degree of suffering should be, we know that it can be much worse depending on your level of grief and your way of thinking about the bad things that have happened to you.

Take heart, because in this world you will have trouble, and your trouble is no worse than all the trouble everyone else in this world is having, and it is nothing that you can't handle. That's biblical, so we know it's true. (Wanna check? Read John

16:33.) In this world you are gonna have trouble, and that's why we wrote *Over It*—because there is no one on earth who doesn't have something they need to get over. **At the fall of man we were all given an equal portion of original sin**. That means we're all capable of the same messed-up things, so welcome to the club. There aren't any of us without any problems whatsoever; there just aren't. So if you are human and you are breathing, then guess what? You're in for it.

What's Your Problem?

Is there anything in your life you can't stop thinking about? Anything anyone has said or done, any mistake you have made, any unkind word, any abuse, any backstabbing or frontstabbing? Is there anything causing you to feel embarrassment, shame, bitterness, anger, fear, worry, depression, or guilt? Then you have something you need to get over. You might hear something insignificant about your hair or your clothes and spend the rest of the day stewing over it, dissecting it, and wondering what in the world that person meant. Or you might find out someone told someone else something about you that was totally false—not a huge deal, but a total lie—and you might spend the next week unable to get over thinking about it. If there is something, anything, no matter how big or how small, that draws you into sin by making you doubt, fear, worry, or do anything else that God commands you not to do, then it's time to get over it.

Getting over it is not only good for you; it's right for you. That's because anything that you can't get over becomes an idol. Look at it like this: one definition of idolatry is "an immoderate attachment or devotion to something." "But I don't have an idol!" you protest. Certainly not, not one made out of gold or wood or anything. But you do have an obsession—something you can't get over, something you think about all the time, something that controls you and makes you sick, tired, stressed, worried, and fearful. And have you ever considered what an obsession is? Check out Webster's definition of the word: "a persistent disturbing preoccupation with an often unreasonable idea or feeling." Sound familiar?

Just for kicks, let's take a look at those two definitions side by side. Sure, why not? It might help.

idolatry: an immoderate attachment or devotion to something

obsession: a persistent disturbing preoccupation with an often unreasonable idea or feeling

In other words, in both cases you have an immoderate or persistent attachment or preoccupation with something other than God. Do you need to get over that? If you say you believe in God and his promises according to his words written in the Bible, then yes, you need to get over it! In fact, we could say, based on this knowledge, that whatever you can't get over is bringing you down spiritually. It's sapping your strength and getting you off track. It's keeping you from the promises of God. It's keeping you down, slowing you down, and messing you up. You know it, you feel it, and you want it gone. So it's no wonder you've picked up this book.

We can relate. We've had so many things in our lives that have needed getting over. Some have been quick to go, but others have taken us a lifetime so far. So we aren't calling you out here and putting a scarlet letter on your chest or anything. We're saying we've been there, done that. We know that of which we speak, and it ain't good! And what kind of people would we be if we knew the cure for cancer but didn't share it with the rest of the world?

That's really what we have here—a cancer of the soul, a toxic growth that threatens your spiritual and emotional life. For people who don't have the cure, this might be a death sentence, or at very least require a long, drawn-out series of experimental drugs and

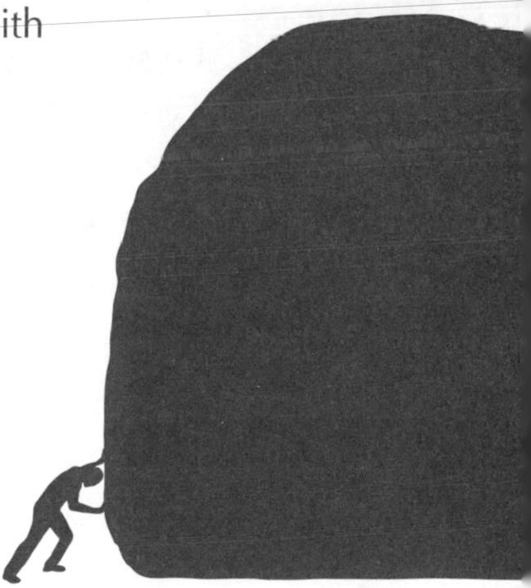

treatments, but you are in luck because we have a cure that's not only effective but swift. It will remove this abnormal growth on your soul faster than any laser or radiation treatment ever could. And it's all based on love.

All this talk about cancer might sound ridiculous, but just think about it a minute. That thing you have failed to get over has attached itself to you. And what has that attachment gotten you? People who can't get over the things they should get over deal with just as many symptoms as the cancer patient, if not more. The American Cancer Society lists on its website some general signs and symptoms of cancer. None of these give a surefire diagnosis of cancer, but they may be the result of having cancer. Keep in mind that a symptom is a sign that something is wrong inside you. You might be the only one who knows it's there, but when you notice a symptom, it's smart to attempt to figure out what it might mean. And knowing what some of the symptoms of a thing are can help you identify if you really do have a problem.

So to keep with the analogy of idolatry being like a cancer, let's take a look at the symptoms that may be the result of not being able to get over something in your life. Do any of these apply to you?

insomnia	fatigue	anxiety
envy	angry outbursts	loneliness
fear	worry	hate
bitterness	fights	jealousy
shame	foggy thinking	inability to concentrate
depression	weakness	nervous breakdowns
cutting	eating disorders	addiction

If you suffer from any of these, there might be something in you that is currently out of whack. And we can probably safely say that you'd like it to be gone. And so would we. Getting over things isn't a surefire way to heal yourself of all that ails you, but not getting over something is a surefire way to be "ailed." So if you want to get to the bottom of your soul issues and find out what obsesses you and how to be healed of it, then let the surgery begin!

Knowledge Heals

You can get over a lot of the things in your life with just a little chunk of knowledge. A lot of the things that haunt you and mess with your life are based on lies—not lies that you purposefully tell yourself but lies that you think are the truth. So in an effort to help you get over it, we suggest that shining some light on your lies will make a humongous difference. After all, what good is basing your life on a lie? How can you expect to get anywhere when you think that driving in the right-hand lane is wrong and you should be driving in the left-hand lane? (Caution: Residents of the UK, the Bahamas, and other nations with left-lane driving, reverse this analogy!) If what you believe to be true is really wrong, then it's no wonder your life is full of stress and angst. Lies never make for a productive or growing life. They keep you stuck where you are and don't help you move toward anything of value. So the first step in getting over it is getting head and heart knowledge.

The biggest piece of head knowledge that will help you is the knowledge that the Bible is totally, one hundred percent true. If we can convince you of that statement, then we can help you to get over literally anything. And the biggest heart knowledge you can gain from the Bible is that nothing can separate you from the love of God that is in Christ

Know Meekness

Understanding the life of Jesus gives you knowledge about the trials in your own life. The Bible talks a lot about meekness and humility, two traits of Jesus, and calls believers to make them part of their lives (see Matt. 11:29; 18:4; John 13:1–20; Eph. 4:2). There is great value in understanding these two concepts and making them a part of your life and faith. In the *New Bible Dictionary*, being meek is described like this: "The meek do not resent adversity because they accept everything as being the effect of God's wise and loving purpose for them, so that they accept injuries from men also, knowing that these are permitted by God for their ultimate good." When you have the knowledge of God and understand why he lets things happen to you that on the surface seem to be really, really bad, you are free from the bondage of the past. You can know that any failure or any bad thing that has happened in your life turns out for your good and not your destruction.

Jesus—not angels or demons, not the present or the future, not any power, not death or life or anything else in all creation (look at Rom. 8:38–39). Nothing can separate you from the most amazing love in the entire universe. That means that nothing, nothing, *nothing* can get between you and what that power has to offer: peace, hope, rest, love, comfort, knowledge, and truth. There's nothing in this world that you can't get over and nothing that can separate you from what is yours, the comfort and love of God. For your guilt, pain, or weakness, we're offering you knowledge. And in every case, with that knowledge of God's Word, you can get over it all!

Whatever it is that keeps you in bondage, that keeps you stuck in the past, repeating the same scene over and over again in your mind, it can be taken away. It's taken away the same way that sin is taken away: by giving it to Jesus. His blood redeems not only your sin but also your pain, your suffering, and your past.

The World's Biggest Failure

Have you ever considered the fact that at the point when the disciples saw Jesus Christ crucified, his life was a complete failure in everyone's mind but God's? All that he'd said and all that he'd done seemed to be a complete waste, even a lie. His followers' hearts were broken. Tears were shed. Disciples walked away dejected. How could this man who had shown such promise and who did so many miracles now be dying a horrible and seemingly useless death? To the world looking on, the cross was a hideous end. But after three days of grieving they saw differently, and suddenly God's plan became clear. Their hearts saw the truth and their lives changed. They looked beyond the circumstance that had paralyzed them and saw behind it into God's plan. **Anytime you can catch a glimpse of God's plan, you are set free, and so were the disciples—set free to believe and to trust.**

In this life you are bound to have problems. You are bound to want what you can never have. You are going to get hurt, to fall down, to cry, to rage. You are going to have moments of loneliness and despair. You are going to feel rejected and disdained. And if you see only what is in front of you, then you, like the disciples, might lose faith. You might wonder where God went. You might question his existence or his love. But if you can see beyond the surface, if you can find the truth in the moment, then you can rise above and not only survive it but flourish in it.

"God is love" (1 John 4:8 NIV). In him there is nothing bad, nothing evil, nothing worthless or vile. He is everything you've ever wanted and anything you've ever needed. To those who know God and have made him Lord of their lives, there is always hope. And that is because no matter how bad things get, they always know there is something far greater going on behind the scenes. The true believer is sure that God is who he says he is and because of that he can be trusted with anything—even the dark, ugly, scary things.

That all adds up to one important fact: there is nothing on this earth that you cannot get over. But maybe that idea doesn't sit well with you. Maybe you like holding on to the past. Maybe it comforts you and keeps you warm. Maybe it defines you. Maybe being free from it seems unfathomable. That's understandable. Like we said at the beginning of this, your past in many ways defines you. It's the outline of the paths you have taken, the roads you have walked, and good or bad, it has made you who you are. And so forgetting that past, or getting over it, might seem like a betrayal of who you are. Okay, we get that. It makes sense, and we can relate on some level as well. We too have defined ourselves by our past.

For Hayley it's been about who she is as a girl. Through high school and college and into her working years, she was plagued by mean girls. These girls despised her and did all they could to make her life miserable. Girls talked about her, spread rumors about her, hung nooses in her locker, spit on her car every day of the week, TP'd her house, gave her

"The climax of sin is that it crucified Jesus Christ, and what was true in the history of God on earth will be true in your history and in mine."

—OSWALD CHAMBERS, *MY UTMOST FOR HIS HIGHEST*

undeservedly bad reviews at work, excluded her from parties, and kept her an outsider. Because of them Hayley decided that girls were no good and unessential for life, and she moved on to boys. Men made more sense to her. They weren't so emotional, catty, or vindictive. They liked her for who she was and weren't jealous or petty around her. So her life became defined by something she couldn't get over: mean girls. And for a bunch of years she spent her life without any feminine relationships at all (except some friendships with girly guys). Sure, the guys were great, but there is something about a girl that only another girl can ever truly understand. And for many years Hayley missed out on that.

But the story didn't end there. When Hayley applied the knowledge of God's Word to her feelings on the girls in her life, she discovered some lies she had been believing; namely, that God wasn't anywhere in the equation and that nothing good could come from it. She had been missing out on the truth that God has a lot to say about enemies and how he wants his children to deal with them. She learned that the pain in her life had a grand purpose she had been missing all those years. Once she discovered that, she was suddenly able to get over it. And at that point her life took a dramatic change. The stress, worry, and fear associated with people of the same sex went away. She no longer sat waiting for their next attack or expecting them to reject her. Instead, she proceeded as God had intended—in love, in hope, and in faith that he would work it all together for good, no matter how ugly things got. And so when she wrote the book *Mean Girls*, out of her pain and suffering came help for hundreds of thousands of young women the world over who were dealing with the same kinds of issues and couldn't get over it.

For Michael, his lifelong obsession was to get married young and have kids before he got old. That was because his parents had him late in life and weren't like all his friends' parents. He couldn't play sports or wrestle around with his dad or have an active life with his parents. So Michael was determined to find love early in his life so that his kids wouldn't have to have the same disappointments. He just couldn't get over his "loss" of having older parents. So he got married early in his twenties, without making a serious commitment to his faith or seeking a spouse who sought after God above all else. Less than three years later, that marriage was over. That just led him further into a desperate spiral of "love first, God second"—an obsession

that he finally surrendered to God a year before meeting Hayley. And since then he's co-written a number of relationship books with Hayley that have helped other people avoid (or heal from) making the mistakes he made.

All this to say, we've done our fair share of obsessing over the past and the sin of others. We've reacted both the way the world said we should and the way God calls us to, and we've found out that God's way works! In fact, it runs circles around the world's ways. So before you shut this book, never to return to it again, give us a chance to shed a little light on the lies you've been believing and give you a little hope and healing for the pain and suffering you've been living in at your own hands. You can get *Over It*, we promise!

"To dwell on the past simply causes ***failure*** in the present. While you are sitting down and bemoaning the past and regretting all the things you have not done, you are ***crippling*** yourself and preventing yourself from working in the present. Is that Christianity? Of course it is **NOT**."

Martyn Lloyd-Jones, *Spiritual Depression*

Chapter 2

OVER THE

GUILT

"Guilt upon the ***conscience***, like rust upon iron, both defiles and ***consumes*** it, ***gnawing*** and creeping into it, as that does which at last eats out the very heart and substance of the **METAL**."

Bishop Robert South

What Is Guilt?

Guilt is not a good feeling. It can haunt you day and night. It can make your gut ache and your blood pressure race. Guilt is a heavy burden; it wears you down with its continual accusations, pointing a finger at your weaknesses, your blunders, your mistakes, and your failures. Guilt is a cruel taskmaster. When you feel guilty, you can lose all your strength and just want to give up ever trying again. ***Guilt can drive you crazy.*** In fact, it can change not only how you feel but how you think. People consumed with guilt don't think very highly of themselves. And a lot of times, when they don't deal with the guilt in the right way, they start to become a slave to it, doing whatever it tells them to do, as if obeying it will somehow take it away. But obeying guilt never helped anybody. Feeling guilty is most often just plain destructive.

But what is guilt, really? For a lot of people guilt is just that feeling of shame you get when you think you've done something to hurt someone, even if you really haven't. But sometimes feelings of guilt are accurate accusations that you did something wrong,

like a red flag waving, saying, "Don't go any farther! You're way off! Time to stop off-roading and get back on the track."

Whether you are having feelings of guilt because you did something wrong or just because you imagine you did, you can get over it with just a little bit of knowledge. So what do you need to know that will soothe your guilt? Let's see if we can't spell it out.

First off, know that guilt has a lot of names. You might call it embarrassment, shame, regret, sorrow, or even disgrace. Any of those things can feel like guilt. Second, the feeling of guilt can come from lots of different places. You can feel guilty for doing something wrong, for hurting someone, or just for letting someone down. You can feel guilty for missing out on something big you wish you could have been a part of, or you can feel guilty for sinning. Your past sins, bad choices, failures, embarrassments, and regrets can all make you feel guilty. There are so many things you can feel guilty for, it's no wonder that so many of us deal with guilt. But is all guilt created equal? And are we just stuck with it? Let's take a closer look at the different kinds of guilt you might feel and what God has to say about it all.

Good Guilt versus Bad Guilt

Okay, let's just get this straight at the beginning: there are two kinds of guilt. There's good guilt and there's bad guilt. We want you to understand the difference so you can get rid of the bad and know what to do with the good. So here's the bird's-eye view of guilt.

Good guilt is when you do something wrong (i.e., sinful) and you feel responsible for it, and that feeling makes you want to come clean and stop doing what you're doing. Good guilt leads you to God and to his forgiveness that's already bought and paid for, plain and simple. And that's what makes it good. It stops a bad thing and starts up a good thing. It stops the sin and it starts the worship.

But bad guilt is the complete opposite. Bad guilt happens in two situations: (1) when you do something you feel bad about even though it wasn't wrong (i.e., you didn't sin), and (2) when you do something wrong and it leads you not to God but away from him. Bad guilt can make you feel condemned when you are not, and it always leads you away from God. In other words, we're talking about the guilt that leads you *to* sin, not away from it.

The difference might be kind of hard to see right now, so let's see if we can't make it all more obvious. Let's start off with good guilt.

Good Guilt

Good guilt is also known as conviction. It's the feeling you get when what you do doesn't agree with what you know you should be doing—when you sin and you are aware of your wrongdoing. It's a normal part of life, because that feeling is meant for our good, to drive us to fix things and to get back on the right track. It also reminds us who we are and whose we are. Paul talks about his feelings of good guilt in Romans 7. Here is just a peek at the chapter:

> I don't realize what I'm doing. I don't do what I want to do. Instead, I do what I hate. I don't do what I want to do, but I agree that God's standards are good. So I am no longer the one who is doing the things I hate, but sin that lives in me is doing them. I know that nothing good lives in me; that is, nothing good lives in my corrupt nature. Although I have the desire to do what is right, I don't do it. I don't do the good I want to do. Instead, I do the evil that I don't want to do. (Rom. 7:15–19)

Good guilt comes when you don't do what you want to do and you hate what you do. It's when your actions are out of whack with your belief in what is right and wrong, and it's a horrible feeling. These feelings of guilt, or conviction, can really mess with you when you don't know what they are there for. They can even make you question your faith: "Am I really so weak that I can't do what God asks me to do? Am I even saved if I can't do what I know I should?" So let us clear this up: conviction isn't there to condemn you. That's what you need to know. How do we know? We kept reading. Paul ends his discussion on his guilt like this:

> What a miserable person I am! Who will rescue me from my dying body? I thank God that our Lord Jesus Christ rescues me! So I am obedient to God's standards with my mind, but I am obedient to sin's standards with my corrupt nature. So those who are believers in Christ Jesus can no longer be condemned. (Rom. 7:24–8:1)

Did you get it? The big, important part? The life-saving part? "There is now *no* condemnation for those who are in Christ Jesus" (Rom. 8:1 NIV, emphasis added). Phew! That's the biggest relief ever, huh? So this means that good guilt isn't there to condemn you but to do something else. So what's it for?

Paul explains it later in 2 Corinthians like this: "Godly sorrow brings repentance that leads to salvation and leaves no regret" (2 Cor. 7:10 NIV). Okay, "godly sorrow" here means "good guilt." That means that you know your feelings of guilt are good when they bring you to repentance and leave you with no regret. Guilt was meant to be your guide, the warning sign on the road of life, the flashing red light telling you that the bridge is out and to look out for the huge cliff ahead. John Calvin explains it by saying that only those "who have learned well to be earnestly dissatisfied with themselves, and to be confounded with shame at their wretchedness" truly understand the gospel. This kind of shame or guilt is the shame that transforms a life. And it is good guilt.

But there is another kind of good guilt that is more subtle and therefore more easily ignored, and that is subconscious guilt or, as we like to call it, gut guilt. In this situation you aren't sure if you've messed up or not, but you have a hunch that maybe what you did was bad. It's kind of a gut feeling. You feel like you've done something wrong, but you aren't sure because you don't know God's Word well enough. This kind of conviction should make you want to learn more to find out if you've messed up.

When Hayley was younger she believed the Bible, and so she believed that sex before marriage was a sin. But then she met a guy who said he was a Christian who asked her, "If God created sex, then why wouldn't he want us to have it?" His argument actually sounded right because she didn't really know the Bible at all. She had just heard secondhand what it said and hadn't read any of it or learned any of it for herself. So his words made sense in light of her feelings for the guy, and she fell for them. She went further than she should have, even though she had the terrible feeling that what he said may not have been the truth. She had nothing to back it up, but she had a guilty feeling in her gut that would not let go of her. She didn't set out to sin; she didn't even think she was sinning at the time, because she was so convinced that his argument made sense—but sin is sin no matter what you are thinking at the time. So she felt the sting of guilt, and in the end she was devastated. But this sting is a good sting, because once again this good gut guilt is a sign that God hasn't given up on you but is calling you closer to him.

The Purpose of Good Guilt

> When he comes, he will convict the world concerning sin and righteousness and judgment. (John 16:8 ESV)

When you feel the pangs of guilt because the Holy Spirit convicts you of doing something wrong, it won't be your relationships with other humans that you're worried about but your relationship with God. Certainly there will be some regret for what you did to someone else, but your main concern isn't what they think of you or what you have done to them; your main concern is what you have

done to God and what he thinks of you. Guilt is meant to convict you of sin, because sin is something you do to God. People might be the recipients of your sin, but ultimately all sin is against God. That's why even nonbelievers experience guilt. According to the Bible, "They demonstrate that God's law is written in their hearts, for their own conscience and thoughts either accuse them or tell them they are doing right" (Rom. 2:15 NLT). Guilt isn't evidence of a right relationship with God; it is the realization that your relationship with God needs attention. You have to understand that so you can get out from under the guilt that convicts you.

When you sense the conviction of sin or a feeling of guilt, remember where that comes from, and don't confuse that with other people's reactions or conviction. John 12:43 describes people who let what others think guilt them into action or inaction, when it is only the conviction of God that ought to dictate our actions: "For they loved human praise more than praise from God" (NIV). When what people say or think about you is more important to you than what God thinks about you, you start feeling bad for all kinds of things that aren't sin. Michael struggled through most of his twenties and thirties feeling guilty if he wasn't a "people pleaser." That's why he made some silly and downright stupid decisions in his relationships at school, at work, and with the opposite sex. Michael felt guilty if

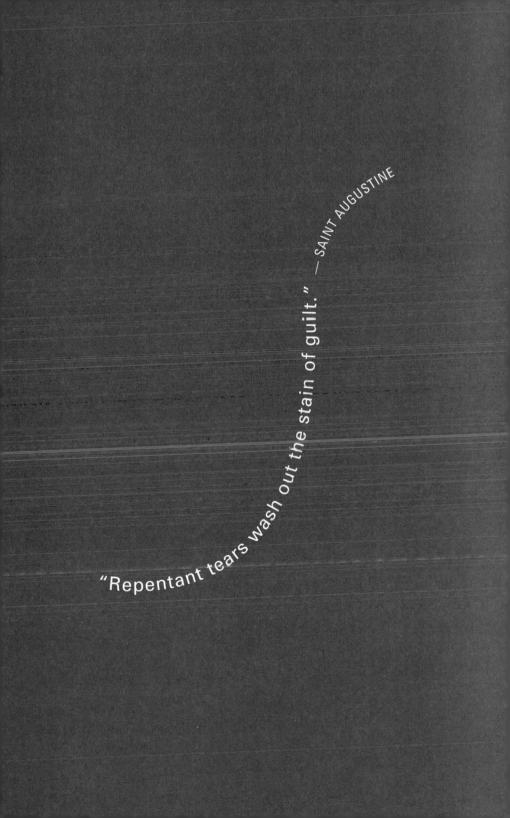

"Repentant tears wash out the stain of guilt." — SAINT AUGUSTINE

he didn't make people happy, and that just led to other stupid decisions and made him and others around him the opposite of happy. That's because God's main purpose for guilt isn't social change but spiritual change.

Don't let guilt be just an inconvenient experience. Get to the bottom of it through studying God's Word and understanding the purpose or source of the guilt that you are experiencing. As a believer you have to respond to your guilt by agreeing with God that you are guilty of breaking his law and asking for his help in never doing it again. Then, after you've done that, get over it. Guilt is meant to redirect your steps—once its work is done, you can and should get rid of it (more on this later).

Good Reasons to Feel Guilty

Before we dive into the bad reasons for guilt, we want to give you a quick reference list of reasons for good guilt so you'll be able to know which is which. Here are some things that *should* give you that feeling of guilt or conviction because you have broken God's law. The only cause of good guilt is sin. That's the overarching category for all of the things that follow. But maybe you don't know God's law as well as you should, and maybe you aren't sure where the line is drawn, so here are a few examples of sin and how it convicts.

Disobeying authority—When you are told to do something by someone who is in charge of you and you don't do it, you don't just disobey them; you disobey God, who put them in authority over you. So even if what they said seems stupid, you still should have feelings of guilt for being disobedient to God. Of course, this doesn't mean that you do what you are told to do even if it's a sin. Sin is never meant to be an option for a believer—not even when those in authority over you insist on it.

Not wanting to discover your own sin—If you had some glorious sin in your life that you loved, would you rather stay blissfully unaware that it was sin or have it pointed out? Ignorance, according to God's Word, is not bliss. In 1 Corinthians 15:34 Paul tells believers to "Come back to the right point of view, and stop sinning. Some people don't know anything about God. You should be ashamed of yourselves." It's not a get-out-of-jail-free card to say, "But I didn't know." He's your God, and it's your job to find out what pleases him (see 2 Cor. 5:9; Eph. 5:10). Don't just let stuff slide when you feel guilty, saying, "Well, I'm not even sure it's a sin." Get the facts.

Complaining about discipline—"If you reject discipline, you only harm yourself; but if you listen to correction, you grow in understanding" (Prov. 15:32 NLT). Discipline comes when you mess up and do something wrong. And it can come from someone in authority over you, and that includes

God. Either way, when you complain about it you only harm yourself. That means getting over it is the smart choice. When you whine and complain about it, it is not only uncomfortable but unprofitable. Ugh—what a waste of discipline.

Blaming God—When bad stuff happens, it's easy to blame God. After all, he could have saved you. But blaming God just makes you guilty of being foolish. Job's wife tried to get her husband to blame God when bad things were happening. But Job said to her, "You're talking like a godless fool. We accept the good that God gives us. Shouldn't we also accept the bad?" (Job 2:10). When you are angry with God, it's natural to want to blame him and turn your back. His ways aren't your ways, so even if you have no idea why he allowed this bad thing to happen, you have to trust that if he's allowed it, it's for your best. So get over the blame game, and trust that his ways are the best ways. If he didn't rescue you from something, it was for your good. That can be hard to believe, but it is true (see Rom. 8:28).

Being prideful—Pride is the foundation of all sin, the beginning of it all. So feeling a twinge of guilt for being proud is good guilt and should be listened to. If you don't, it will not end well for you because "Pride ends in humiliation, while humility brings honor" (Prov. 29:23 NLT).

Not listening—"You're not listening to me!" Ever heard that or said that? Not listening, according to the Bible, is a reason to feel bad. "Whoever gives an answer before he listens is stupid and shameful" (Prov. 18:13). So if you haven't listened, then your shame is good—use it for that and start paying attention to what people say. (Perhaps you should reread this paragraph just in case you weren't listening.)

Being proud of the wrong things you do—Nothing says it better than this: "In the end they will be destroyed. Their own emotions are their god, and they take pride in the shameful things they do. Their minds are set on worldly things" (Phil. 3:19).

Lying—No one needs to tell you that lying is wrong. It's something everyone seems to know, whether they believe in God or not. If you feel guilt for lying, then you've got some good guilt. Take the guilt and let it lead you to stop the lies. "A righteous person hates lying, but a wicked person behaves with shame and disgrace" (Prov. 13:5).

The list could go on and on, but we think you probably get the picture. Sin is a reason for good guilt. If you are feeling guilty, find out if what you did was a sin or not, and if it was a sin, then you know what to do next, don't you? Confess your sin, repent, stop doing it, and start obeying God.

Bad Guilt

In a life without faith, guilt is a bad thing. It convicts with no chance at parole or acquittal. And no

Good Guilt

Good guilt is when you feel guilty for doing something wrong and the guilt makes you want to come clean and stop doing what you're doing. Good guilt leads you to God.

Bad Guilt

Bad guilt is when you feel guilty for doing something even though you didn't sin. Bad guilt makes you feel condemned when you are not and leads you away from God.

one wants anything to do with it. For nonbelievers, guilt seems unnecessary because all it does is cause a load of pain that has no real meaning other than reminding them of their mistakes. And since "mistake" is a relative term, guilt is a waste of time.

But when are feelings of guilt a bad thing for the believer? In other words, when do you say no to that nudge of guilt and when do you freely accept it? When the guilt you are feeling is misplaced—when it is guilt not over sin but over failure, suffering, mistakes, embarrassment, or a missed opportunity—then it's bad guilt. Guilt was meant to convict of sin and not of anything else. So when a person feels guilty because they underdressed for a job interview or guilty for not remembering everything on the shopping list, it's bad guilt. We cannot be held spiritually guilty of relational faux pas. We may be embarrassed or regretful of them, but we are not guilty.

Sin is going against God's will, not going against another person's will. In order to be guilty before God, you have to go against his will. When someone tries to convince you that you are guilty because you went against *their* human will, they are pressuring you with bad guilt. The exception, of course, is if it is part of God's will that you obey that person's will, like with parents or police (see Eph. 6:1; 1 Pet. 2:13–17). In that case it's really still the same: your sin isn't that you broke from their will but that you broke from God's.

The Two Kinds of Bad Guilt

As we see it, there are two different kinds of bad guilt. The first one is the feeling you get when what you feel guilty about doing wasn't sinful at all. It's when you judge something in your past or your actions as bad even though God doesn't judge it that way. When you feel guilty for that, you are essentially letting society or emotions be your judge instead of God. And if God doesn't consider what you did a sin, why do you? This kind of guilt makes humans more important than God, and guess what—the Bible has something to say about that. It's in Galatians 1:10, which is a great verse to memorize and think of whenever you start to feel guilty because of breaking a human's will and not God's. It goes like this: "Obviously, I'm not trying to win the approval of people, but of God. If pleasing people were my goal, I would not be Christ's servant" (NLT). When you feel bad guilt, it's because you are trying to please people. And that's gonna backfire, because the old saying is true: "You can please some of the people some of the time, but you can't please all of the people all of the time." So the real sin that should make you feel guilty is obsessing over the guilt of not pleasing people, not that you went against what they wanted.

The second feeling of bad guilt is the feeling that you hold on to when you have actually sinned but then confessed and repented—and then basically refused God's gift of forgiveness. In this situation you hold on to those feelings of good guilt longer than you should because you don't believe that God is really big enough or good enough to do what he says, and that is to forgive you. You may have never heard it put like that, but when you say things like "I just can't forgive myself" or "God can never forgive me," you disagree with God. Good guilt, like bananas, has a shelf life. Hold on to it too long and it starts to turn brown and gross. See, God says to confess and you will be forgiven (see 1 John 1:9), so if you confess but say you *aren't* forgiven, you are calling him a liar. And that makes for bad guilt. A sin confessed is a guilt taken away. Period. The end. And when you hold on to feelings of guilt when the guilt is gone, you waste grace and God's kindness.

Bad Reasons to Feel Guilty

You've got to get over the bad guilt. Bad guilt is not meant to be held on to but to be confessed, because it is a sin. In case you still aren't sure if your feelings of guilt are bad or good, here are a few examples of bad guilt to think about.

Guilt for not doing what your friends are doing— One of the most popular guilts is the guilt you

feel when your friends get on you for obeying God. It can be easy to feel guilty about stuff like not going someplace your friends are going or doing something they are doing that is against God's law. You can feel bad for "flaking out" on them because you said you would go but then you realized that it just wouldn't be right. But that bad guilt you feel for living for Christ is just fake shame. God's Word says so in Psalm 25:3: "No one who hopes in you will ever be put to shame" (NIV).

Guilt for saying no to someone you love—A lot of believers, especially girls, can feel a bad sense of guilt when they say no, like saying no to a guy who wants them to prove their love to him or saying no to friends who want them to join in on revenge or talking bad about someone. Even for guys who want to be the hero and save the day, saying no to people you care about can make you feel bad guilt. But trusting God and doing his will is never a cause for guilt. "As it is written, 'Behold, I am laying in Zion a stone of stumbling, and a rock of offense; and whoever believes in him will not be put to shame' " (Rom. 9:33 ESV).

Guilt for sharing your faith—Bad guilt can hit when you share your faith with someone and they are not happy about it or you feel like a fool for doing it. When you are embarrassed by talking about Jesus, that is bad guilt. In 2 Timothy 1:8 Paul tells his readers, "Never be ashamed to tell others about our Lord or be ashamed of me, his prisoner. Instead, by God's power, join me in suffering for the sake of the Good News." There is no shame in talking about Jesus. It's only a shame when you don't.

Guilt for loving Jesus more than anyone else—As believers we are called to make Jesus Lord of our lives, and that means loving him more than anyone else. That's not so hard until someone wants you to love them more than anyone else. In that case what they really want is for you to idolize them. Sometimes boyfriends, girlfriends, best friends, and even spouses can slip into this mode without even knowing it. It's not like they actually demand to be your little god, but when they want you to do whatever they want—in other words, to obey them at all times—then they want to be god. If anyone gets angry because of your allegiance to God, beware of the bad guilt they are trying to inflict. Your love for Christ must overshadow every other love. In Luke 14:26 Jesus says, "If you want to be my disciple, you must hate everyone else by comparison—your father and mother, wife and children, brothers and sisters—yes, even your own life. Otherwise, you cannot be my disciple" (NLT). This means that you should feel absolutely no guilt in loving Jesus the most. Period.

Guilt for failure or weakness—When you fail at doing something, you can easily fall into feelings of bad guilt, blaming yourself for this or that and refusing to get over it. But it's the same story: If you haven't sinned, then what are you guilty of? Breaking your own law? Who are you, a god? Your failure or weakness is not meant to ruin you but to teach you something important. Look at these thoughts from Paul to find out more:

> But he told me: "My kindness is all you need. My power is strongest when you are weak." So I will brag even more about my weaknesses in order that Christ's power will live in me. Therefore, I accept weakness, mistreatment, hardship, persecution, and difficulties suffered for Christ. It's clear that when I'm weak, I'm strong. (2 Cor. 12:9–10)

Biblically speaking, weakness is a cause for bragging, because your weakness and failure allow God to be your strength. Don't get all wrapped up in the discovery that you're a weak and stupid human being—that's not news for anyone, and certainly not us! But God's wisdom and power are all you (and we) need to get over any failure we could ever experience.

Guilt for missing out on something—When you miss out on doing or getting something big, you can easily start to feel regret, or guilt, over not getting what you wanted. And it can be easy to wallow in the misery of it all, but getting over it is the only way of obedience in this situation. You have to get over the fact that God didn't allow you to have something that you wanted. And you have to trust that God's wisdom in this situation is better than yours ever could be. If God wanted you to have that thing, then he would have made sure you got it. The question to ask yourself is, "Would I want something that God didn't think was good for me to have?" Not being able to get over missing out on something is calling God a liar, because he promises to care for you and to do with you what is best. God says to you, " 'For I know the plans I have for you,' says the Lord. 'They are plans for good and not for disaster, to give you a future and a hope' " (Jer. 29:11 NLT). Do you trust him? Then you have to get over it right now.

Guilt for a sin you have confessed—Good guilt turns bad when you confess your sin and then refuse to accept the forgiveness God has given you. Think of it like this: when you sin and God forgives you but you don't accept it, it's like you're sinning all over again and again, because you refuse to take God at his word. And if you sin but are just too afraid to confess because you think what you did was too bad, then you're calling God a bad Father. You're saying, by fearing his kindness and grace, that you believe God isn't good and that his grace isn't for everyone, even though his Word makes it clear that it is. And in fact, his grace has nothing to do with how good you are. Remember what Paul says in Ephesians:

> God, who is rich in mercy, made us alive with Christ even when we were dead in transgressions. . . . For it is by grace you have been saved, through faith—and this is not from yourselves, it is the gift of God—not by works, so that no one can boast. (2:4–5, 8–9 NIV)

Not accepting God's forgiveness is living with bad guilt. So get over it! And accept his forgiveness.

Embarrassment for doing something stupid—When you mess up, it can be totally humiliating. You can feel angry at yourself and even have bad guilt over doing something you "shouldn't have." But if what you did wasn't a sin, then the guilt you feel for it is bad. For the believer humiliation isn't a bad thing; it's a constructive thing. It reminds us that we are sinners and deserve punishment, but God has redeemed us. Humility is the foundation of all righteousness, so never let guilt taint an opportunity to experience humiliation and to grow closer to Christ because of it. "Fear of the Lord teaches wisdom; humility precedes honor" (Prov. 15:33 NLT).

Every case of bad guilt is a chance to get over it. Holding on to the world's idea of right and wrong, or your own, is turning your back on God. But living a life knowing the difference between bad guilt and good guilt sets you free and draws you closer to the God of the universe. Remember, there is no condemnation for those who are in Christ Jesus (see Rom. 8:1), so why are you condemning yourself with bad guilt? Get over it! Knowing what you now know will set you free, but only if you are willing to loosen the chains. Any bondage you are in under bad guilt is under your own control. That's good news, guys! It means no one has you in chains but *you*. No one holds the key but *you*. So take the key *you* hold and open those locks. You are free. Bad guilt no more! Let it go today and get on with truth and hope. The future is yours when you refuse to let "guilty" be your identity.

Getting Over the Guilt

We all deal with guilt, and most of the time for good reason. In fact, the Bible backs this up. As Romans

3:23 says, "All people have sinned, they have fallen short of God's glory." And Romans 3:10–12 says, "No one is righteous—not even one. No one is truly wise; no one is seeking God. All have turned away; all have become useless. No one does good, not a single one" (NLT). Sound harsh? Actually this should be a relief. It means you aren't alone; we are all equally sinners, equally turning away from God and doing things our own way. So your case is not unique. You aren't a particularly hard case that has no hope. You are just like all the rest of us: broken and in need of repair. And the beauty of all of this is that knowing we are broken, God sent us a repair kit. He sent us a way to make things right, to appease our guilt, and to get over it. If you aren't sure what we are talking about, take a look at Ephesians 2:1–10:

> You were once dead because of your failures and sins. You followed the ways of this present world and its spiritual ruler. This ruler continues to work in people who refuse to obey God. All of us once lived among these people, and followed the desires of our corrupt nature. We did what our corrupt desires and thoughts wanted us to do. So, because of our nature, we deserved God's anger just like everyone else.
>
> But God is rich in mercy because of his great love for us. We were dead because of our failures, but he made us alive together with Christ. (It is God's kindness that saved you.) God has brought us back to life together with Christ Jesus and has given us a position in heaven with him. He did this through Christ Jesus out of his generosity to us in order to show his

> extremely rich kindness in the world to come. God saved you through faith as an act of kindness. You had nothing to do with it. Being saved is a gift from God. It's not the result of anything you've done, so no one can brag about it. God has made us what we are. He has created us in Christ Jesus to live lives filled with good works that he has prepared for us to do.

So sure, you are guilty—that shouldn't come as a surprise—but that guilt isn't a life sentence. When you trust in the amazing cleaning power of the blood of Christ, you can become as white as snow, spick-and-span, thanks not to you getting things right but to him setting things right. For the believer guilt has a really easy solution: confession. It's a simple practice prescribed by a kind and merciful God, and it goes like this:

> If we claim we have no sin, we are only fooling ourselves and not living in the truth. But if we confess our sins to him, he is faithful and just to forgive us our sins and to cleanse us from all wickedness. If we claim we have not sinned, we are calling God a liar and showing that his word has no place in our hearts.
>
> My dear children, I am writing this to you so that you will not sin. But if anyone does sin, we have an advocate who pleads our case before the Father. He is Jesus Christ, the one who is truly righteous. He himself is the sacrifice that atones for our sins—and not only our sins but the sins of all the world. (1 John 1:8–2:2 NLT)

All of your guilt—all of it!—can be gone today if you are willing to do one simple thing: agree with God that you sinned. That's what confession is. Then it's done. It is finished. Over. And once it's done, you don't need to hold on to it anymore. If you hold on to it, then you haven't truly given it up and trusted the One who wants to take away your guilt. And at that point you are saying that you are a better steward of your guilt than God is. You are saying you are a better judge and that Jesus's work on the cross for you was a waste of time, unnecessary, because it is ineffective for your particular case. You're saying, "Thanks for the effort, but no thanks. I've got this one covered. I'll just hold on to this guilt until its shelf life is finished. Then maybe I'll move on. Sorry for the inconvenience, God." Wow, no one would really say that, would they? But your failure to get over your sin and to give it to God says just that.

Sorry if that hurt, but it's better to hurt than to carry around guilt that you have not let be covered by the blood of Jesus. Guilt that isn't turned over and covered can lead people to some tragic ends. In fact, the Bible gives us one very vivid account of guilt and the tragedy of not getting over it by trusting God with your forgiveness. His name was Judas. I'm sure you've heard of him. Who hasn't? He will forever be remembered as the traitor against Jesus, the guy who was first a friend but became an enemy. Judas was guilty of betraying Jesus and handing him over to the religious leaders who wanted to kill him. As guilty as guilty can be. Because of that, Judas is

nowadays. In
anything. But
guilty but felt
I did it again"
ng, sickening,
me!" kind of
turning over
eading priests
e. Let's take a

realized that
as filled with
of silver back
have sinned,"
nocent man."
"That's your

down in the
mself. (Matt.

When he real-
was filled with
e priests. And
you see what
e had sinned.
had done and
nnocent man.
priests offered
sin. He threw
e floor, and he

TREE OF LIFE #1
COLUMBIA GORGE PREMIUM OUTLETS
450 NW 257TH WAY, SUITE 344
TROUTDALE, OR 97060
(503) 661-3030
(888) 33BIBLE

1 9780310294030
GODS STORY YOUR STORY 5.97
1 9780800731533
OVER IT : LETTING GOD G 4.97
Sub Total 10.94
Total Due 10.94
BANKCARDS 10.94

Change .00

Signature TOON/TRISHA O

Visa 47****0538
VITAL Approval # 055311 (Swiped)
VITAL Reference # 424222203408
This Transaction # 11596/0
**** Reprint ****
AUG 30, 2014 15:54 1 - MR 45

THANK YOU!
TRISHA TOON
RETURNS WITHIN 30 DAYS WITH RECEIPT.
NO RETURNS ON GREEN TAG ITEMS.
HAVE A BLESSED DAY!

"BUT THOSE WHO HOPE IN THE LORD WILL RENEW THEIR STRENGTH. THEY WILL SOAR ON WINGS LIKE EAGLES: THEY WILL RUN AND NOT GROW WEARY, THEY WILL WALK AND NOT BE FAINT."
-ISAIAH 40:31 NIV

ran out and killed himself. The guilt was so overwhelming that he couldn't bear it. It pushed down on him, it made him sick and shameful, and he wanted a way out.

All of us want a way out from under the guilt. We don't like the way it feels, and we are oftentimes powerless to free ourselves from it. When we know we have sinned and we confess that sin to God, we have one more very important thing to do that Judas failed to do. We have to *get over it*.

In this instance that might sound blasphemous. Get over turning over the Son of God to be killed? How could anyone get over that? And you're right—how could they? But what if Judas, after he had thrown down the thirty pieces of silver, followed Jesus to the cross and begged for forgiveness from the man he had betrayed? Can you picture the scene? We would read not only of a thief hanging next to Jesus being forgiven but also of the Son of God forgiving the friend who gave him up to the authorities. If Judas would have gotten over the immense sickness of guilt and covered his remorse and grief with the certainty of who Jesus was and what his power would offer for sinners—if Judas had sought Christ's help in getting over it—we believe he would not have taken his life but gained it. But since he felt like his guilt was more powerful than his God, he had no other option than to punish himself. Tragedy upon tragedy.

We must never believe that our guilt is too much for God's grace.

But Judas wasn't the only one to betray Jesus. There was another, but his story goes a completely different way. His is the story of a man who turned his back on his friend in order to protect himself. His name was Peter, and he was decidedly one of Jesus's best friends but still turned his back on Jesus out of fear. Three times he was asked by bystanders if he was a friend of Jesus, and three times he said, "I don't know the guy." The betrayal might not seem as damaging as Judas's, but to Peter it was every bit as horrible. In Matthew 26:75 we see what the sudden realization of guilt did to Peter. It caused him to literally run away weeping and sobbing in grief. The guilt was *almost* overwhelming. But Peter's life didn't end the way Judas's did. Peter didn't deem his guilt more powerful than his God, and in the end Peter lived to see the resurrection of his Savior and the establishment of Christ's church.

We must never believe that our guilt is too much for God's grace. We cannot side with Judas, who allowed sin to take his life, when we know that sin doesn't have to be our end. If we are willing to believe God's Word, we no longer have an excuse for holding on to our guilt and refusing to get over it, because God's Word tells us:

> Yet God, with undeserved kindness, declares that we are righteous. He did this through Christ Jesus when he freed us from the penalty for our sins. For God presented Jesus as the sacrifice for sin. People are

made right with God when they believe that Jesus sacrificed his life, shedding his blood. This sacrifice shows that God was being fair when he held back and did not punish those who sinned in times past, for he was looking ahead and including them in what he would do in this present time. God did this to demonstrate his righteousness, for he himself is fair and just, and he declares sinners to be right in his sight when they believe in Jesus. (Rom. 3:24–26 NLT)

Don't let anybody fool you: there is always relief from guilt. Real guilt, the good kind, finds instant relief in the Savior. The first two steps of confession and repentance guarantee freedom from the guilt of our sin. And bad guilt is just as easily tossed out when you realize that you are not guilty of things that are not a sin. That's why understanding the difference between good guilt and bad guilt is essential to getting guilt out of your life. The third step is walking into the promises of God and trusting that his ways, though they are not our ways, are perfect and will always lead you to freedom and peace. Taking these three steps will give you the supernatural leap you need to get over guilt.

Chapter 3

OVER THE

PAIN

"If through a ***broken*** heart God can bring His ***purposes*** to pass in the world, then thank Him for breaking your **HEART**."

Oswald Chambers, *My Utmost for His Highest*

The Source of Pain

Guilt is an uncomfortable feeling, but it's completely different from the feeling we are talking about in this chapter. You experience guilt because of the things done *by* you, while pain comes from the things done *to* you by others or by yourself. Pain can be physical or emotional or both. It can be from something that happened in the past or something that's happening right now. And it can control you. When the pain gets too overwhelming, it's all you can do to function. And sometimes pain can completely cripple you emotionally.

Before we get started, let us just note that there are two different kinds of pain that need to be addressed when learning how to get over it. The first is the pain of the past: bad memories, heartaches, abuse, and bad things that have been done to you. These are things that can hurt you deeply. They may be stomping on your last nerve. They may be threatening to undo you. They may be making you totally depressed. But they are not meant to debilitate you. They are not meant to be the definition of who you are or who you become.

These are things that we want to help you to get over—and not only to get over but to move beyond. When you can look at this kind of pain from God's perspective and see its value and its purpose, then you can get up on the wave of it and ride it like the famous surfer Kelly Slater. Every surfer knows that you have to paddle hard and get on top of the wave in order to have a successful ride. Let the wave overcome you and engulf you, and you're down in an instant. You can ride on the top of the wave as it curls below or surf through the pipe of the wave if it's big enough. But either way, you can't let it be your demise and take you under. You've got to get over it.

But there is a second kind of pain, and this kind of pain is deep and irremovable. It is a pain that is the mother of all pain. This pain isn't just inconvenient; it is life altering. **When you experience a loss so deep that it changes your world, pain seemingly defines you.** We are talking here about the pain of losing someone you love and never seeing them again on this earth, and the pain of disability, such as losing the use of your legs or experiencing chronic suffering where your body relentlessly hurts.

These kinds of physical losses that will never be undone are not the kind of things we are going to tell you to just get over. We are aware that getting over it is something that has its proper time in the area of pain, and for severe physical loss the proper time to get over it may be very far in the future. For example, when a boy loses his father in a car accident, we don't tell him to man up and get over it. That would be irrational and lacking compassion and grace. Suffering isn't something that should be covered up, ignored, or denied. It is the response to pain in our lives, and the depth of that pain will determine, to a great extent, the length of our suffering. Some pain, like losing a parent, is going to take its time in your life.

King David experienced pain that wasn't fleeting and didn't just kinda hurt—it tore into his life like the horns of a bull. David suffered a lot when he was running away from Saul, who wanted to kill him. He had to hide away in caves, fear for his life, and wonder when it would end. His life was flipped upside down as he hid in terror. Pain changed his life, and your pain might be doing the same to you. Look at how David described his pain and suffering:

> Have compassion on me, Lord, for *I am weak*.
> Heal me, Lord, for *my bones are in agony*.
> I am *sick at heart*.
> How long, O Lord, until you restore me? . . .
> I am worn out from sobbing.
> All night I flood my bed with weeping,
> drenching it with my tears. (Ps. 6:2–3, 6 NLT, emphasis added)

O Lord, how long will you forget me?
Forever?
How long will you look the other way?
How long must I struggle with *anguish in my soul*,
with *sorrow in my heart* every day? (Ps. 13:1–2 NLT, emphasis added)

My God, my God, why have you abandoned me?
Why are you so far away when *I groan for help*?
Every day I call to you, my God, but you do not answer.
Every night you hear my voice, but *I find no relief*. (Ps. 22:1–2 NLT, emphasis added)

Pain is real. And pain at the hands of deep suffering isn't something that you have to get over today. Suffering has to run its course, so if your life-changing pain is fresh, then don't think you've got to ignore it or cover it up. That's not true. But let us help you discover how to start working toward finding relief. As we look at the purposes God has for pain and the spiritual awakening that can come out of it, take these words to heart and know that though your pain might seem to have no purpose other than to completely ruin you, that isn't true. Pain has a very good and great purpose in the life of all who have turned their lives over to Jesus.

As with all things in your life, for getting past your pain it is crucial that you understand that nothing happens to you except what God allows for his glory and your ultimate benefit. We know that when it comes to your pain—those things that have hurt you, bruised you, even broken you—it can be hard to see any good coming of it at all, especially when no good is in sight. Pain, like the Grand Canyon, can be a hard thing to get over. But it can be gotten over, even if it is never removed. And figuring out how that happens is what we are going to do in this chapter.

The pain in your life can come from a lot of places, many of which are completely out of your control. We live in a depraved, broken world where people look away from God and do whatever they want, and a lot of times that includes hurting people around them. Hayley's life was turned upside down by an adulterous father. His sexploits plagued her for years and made her feel unloved by the first man in her life. Michael's life went topsy-turvy when his mom left his dad for almost a year, even getting her own apartment, all because she wasn't getting what she wanted out of the marriage and she wanted to make a point. For a

"My suffering was good for me, for it taught me to pay attention to your decrees."

—PSALM 119:71 NLT

little kidlet, that's a painful and incomprehensible point. Our point is, broken people do broken things and sometimes never even realize the effect they are having on others.

Your heart might be broken; your body might be bruised; your feelings might be hurt. Mean people might surround you; offensive people might attack you. You might be dealing with the pain of resentment and anger against your offenders. All this pain can seep into your life and make your future look bleak. Looking at it like this might make you start to think that pain is pretty much inevitable. Live and you're gonna get hurt. And that's pretty much true. Jesus even talked about it when he said, "In this world you *will* have trouble" (John 16:33 NIV, emphasis added). There's no way around it. Live, and trouble will come.

But the amazing thing for the life of the believer is that pain is never the end of the story. In fact, in the life of faith it's just the beginning. Without the pain of the cross endured by Christ, where would your faith be? His pain was your salvation. His suffering was your gift of eternal life.

The Beauty of Pain

Even the most messy and horrible stuff wasn't meant to destroy you but to make you stronger and more holy. Even the biggest pain in your life can be a tool in the hand of the sculptor if you are only willing to stand still and let him do his work. When you can do that, nothing others do can destroy you. Even if they plot against you, attack you, and hate you, you are still hopeful and confident in the One who saves.

God's Word confirms this truth through the story of Joseph's life. This was a guy who knew about pain. He was hated by his brothers, sold into slavery, and put into prison, but still he knew who was in charge. He was certain of it, and in the end he was able to say to his brothers, "Even though you planned evil against me, God planned good to come out of it" (Gen. 50:20).

When pain comes your way, you can follow one of two lines of questioning. One is to ask, "Why me?" It's the natural response to pain and suffering to ask, "What have I done wrong? Why me?" and even "Where was God in all this? Doesn't he care?" These questions make sense to the natural mind, and they are the usual gut response, but they don't usually get you anywhere. The problem is that they are accusatory. They assume that you shouldn't have been the one suffering, and so God must have messed up. This line of questioning is more self-centered than God-centered, so the answers you get never fully satisfy you.

But there is another line of questioning that soothes the believing heart and is at the very least a foundation for getting your ultimate answer.

It begins something like this: "Could God have stopped whatever it is that is making me suffer?" That's a foundational question, and it says a lot about what you believe about God. If you can confidently answer yes, then good for you; you're on the right track. But if you can't answer yes, then you need to learn more about God and what we call his sovereignty, which is his power over the world and everything that happens in it.

Let's take a quick look at Daniel 4:35 and see if it helps you get a better picture:

> Everyone who lives on earth is nothing compared to him. He does whatever he wishes with the army of heaven and with those who live on earth. There is no one who can oppose him or ask him, "What are you doing?"

Did you get that? This is where we see that asking "Why me?" is really a silly exercise. Are you really gonna ask God what he's doing? Really? Sounds silly when you say it like that, doesn't it? But in case you still aren't buying it, here's one more nail in the coffin of doubt from Isaiah 45:7:

> I create the light and make the darkness.
> I send good times and bad times.
> I, the Lord, am the one who does these things. (NLT)

God's Word confirms it: he's got everything under control. Nothing happens to you that you can't bear (see 1 Cor. 10:13) and that isn't meant for good, because we know that God never intends anything for bad.

Okay, if God has everything under control and he didn't stop what led to your pain, why didn't he? Now this kind of question (unlike "Why me?") is powerful. "Why didn't he?" is the beginning of a great discovery. It's the beginning of making use of the pain rather than resenting it and wishing it away. Asking "Why did God let this happen?" is the first step toward getting over it for good. So let's look at some of the reasons why God lets pain and suffering come into your life. Okay? You up for it? If you are, then let's go!

The School of Pain

Here's the thing about pain in the life of the believer: it's for your good. Always. No question (for extra credit, take a look at Ps. 119:71; Col. 1:24). God doesn't waste anything in the life of the person whose heart is bent on serving him and knowing him more. Nothing, not even the pain. Since you know pain happens, why does it surprise you when it happens to you? And worse yet, why do you pull away from it, hate it, and even attack it when you have a God who will use it for good if you will only trust him with it?

As a believer you need never let your pain be wasted or used against you. You waste it when you

"God isn't unable to help us, and He doesn't despise us. He is the ruler of all mankind and the lover of His own people. But through suffering He looks into and searches everyone. He weighs the character of every individual during danger, even death. Therefore, as God is revealed in the fire, so our true selves are revealed in critical moments."

Minucius Felix

ignore it and pretend it doesn't exist. And it is used against you when you let it become your excuse to sin. Sinful responses to pain destroy you, while godly responses uplift you. So what is a godly response to pain? And how do you make use of something that hurts so much?

Good questions. The answers have to do with the reasons why God allows suffering and pain in your life. See, if pain were just a random attack on you—if there were no spiritual reason behind it other than your destruction—then you'd have a reason to be upset and resentful. If pain serves no purpose in the life of faith, then you're right to want to medicate it, cover it up, and avoid the sensation at all costs. But because pain serves a big purpose in the life of faith, you can't do what the rest of the world does and sweep it under the rug or let it pile up on you and destroy you.

No, pain is the coach of character. In fact, pain is the gym class teacher that screams in your ear to keep doing push-ups. It's the ultimate *Biggest Loser* experience. It's the way to having a heart that needs nothing but God and because of that can move mountains. And to endure and get over your pain is to see the value in it and to respect it but not fear it. It is to experience it and not numb it or forget it but let it be your spiritual training. When you do, you will see that the things it can teach you are unbelievably important—things like endurance, character, confidence, joy, hope, and trust (see Rom. 5:3; James 1:2–4).

When you rely on God to redeem your pain and make it something of value rather than destruction, you are then able to completely get over it and get on with life to the full. Because that's why Jesus came, you know—not to destroy you but to give you life to the full (see John 10:10). And in order to have life to the full, you have to get over giving your pain the place of power and control over your life. You have to let go of your need to comfort yourself with anything other than God, including your need to avenge yourself or pity yourself, and get on with the real purposes of pain in your life.

So what is your pain teaching you? **The first subject in the school of pain is endurance.** Endurance just means the ability to handle whatever comes your way. Can you imagine letting nothing shake you? Have you seen people like that? These people have a great peace in their lives. They know something the rest of us don't: that "this too shall pass." They know it from experience because the suffering they have lived to tell about has taught them much.

This is the purpose of pain according to the book of James. Take a look at chapter 1, verse 2:

> Be very happy when you are tested in different ways. You know that such testing of your faith produces endurance. Endure until your testing is over. Then you will be mature and complete, and you won't need anything.

See, this line of testing that leads to endurance gets you to the point of peace in suffering because it teaches you through repetition who God is when you need him. The more you suffer, the more he becomes your everything.

In the Western world we really know little of suffering, but in a lot of places where Christians are persecuted, suffering is an active and powerful part of life. Take a look at the lives of people of faith in those dark countries where believers are hated, tortured, starved, and killed, and you will find more power, peace, hope, and patience than you have ever seen. A missionary friend of ours tells the story of pastors in China who consider prison to be their "seminary." That's because, they believe, it is only in suffering for your faith that you truly begin to own it and to have experiences of God's saving power that you can share with others. The persecuted ("suffering") church knows more about the hope and the power of God than most of us in the Western church will ever know because he is all they have, and faith in him demands everything of them—even their lives.

That leads us to another subject in the school of pain: compassion. As Paul says in 2 Corinthians 1:4–5:

> He comforts us whenever we suffer. That is why whenever other people suffer, we are able to comfort them by using the same comfort we have received from God. Because Christ suffered so much for us, we can receive so much comfort from him.

How would you know how to reach out to others, to have compassion on them, and to comfort them if you hadn't experienced the same comfort in your life? We learn from example, and in your pain and suffering God is your example of compassion. As you suffer and look to God for your peace, you learn more about who he is than you could any other way. His Word becomes alive to you. It suddenly makes sense where it didn't before. It ministers to you so that you can minister to others with those same words. If you want your pain to mean something, then know beyond a shadow of a doubt that it all means something big and very important to your life and the kingdom of God. Nothing is just dumb luck. Your pain most certainly will be a step in the direction of a deeper faith and stronger compassion for others who suffer.

Suffering isn't something new. It isn't something rare, and it isn't just reserved for us sinners. Christ himself suffered, and in reading about his suffering

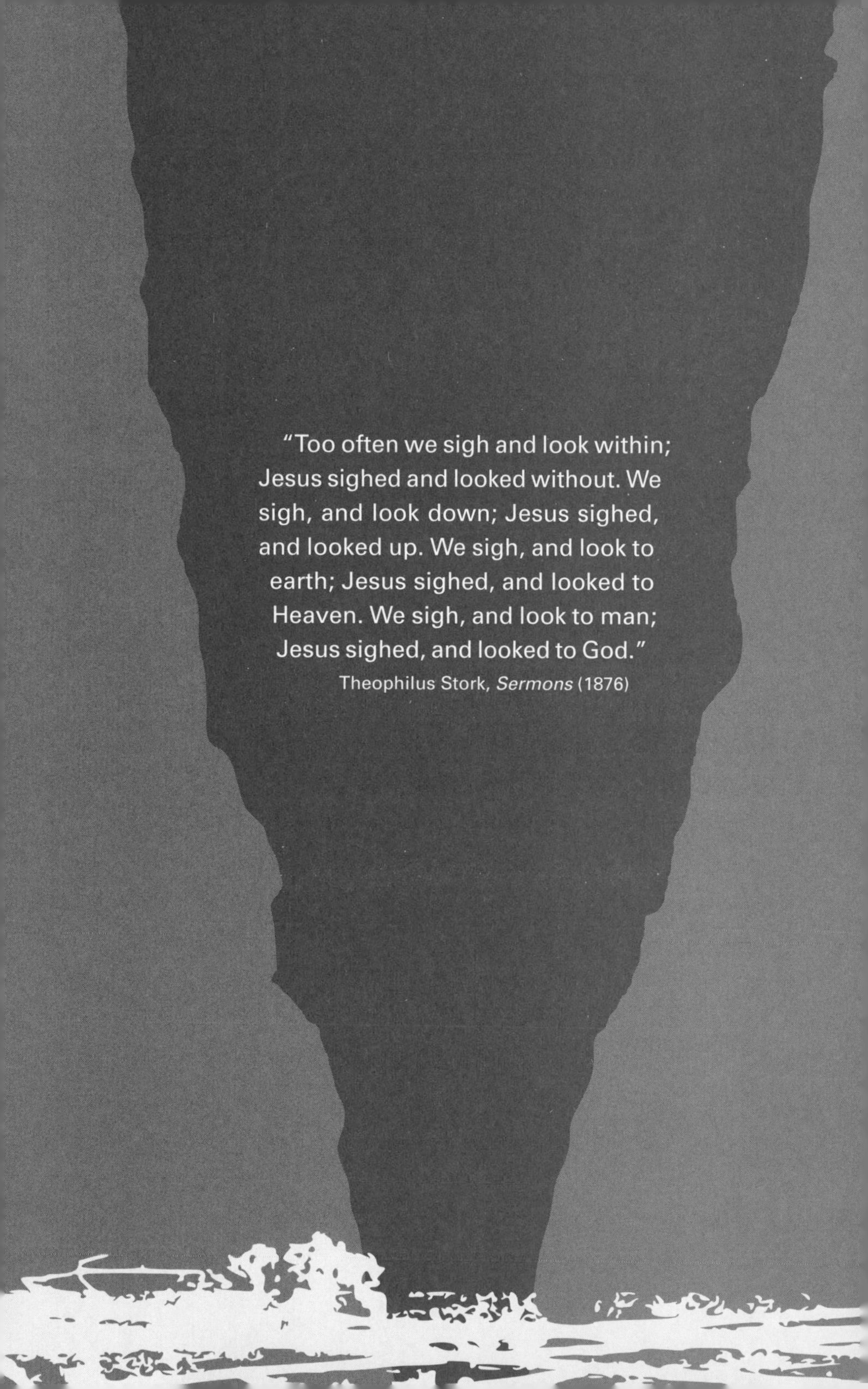

"Too often we sigh and look within; Jesus sighed and looked without. We sigh, and look down; Jesus sighed, and looked up. We sigh, and look to earth; Jesus sighed, and looked to Heaven. We sigh, and look to man; Jesus sighed, and looked to God."

Theophilus Stork, *Sermons* (1876)

you can learn another important lesson about pain. Hebrews 5:8 says, "Although Jesus was the Son of God, he learned to be obedient through his sufferings." Obedience isn't what saves you, but it is what proves you know Christ (see 1 John 2:3), and in suffering your obedience is proven in a major way. **Suffering is the hardest place for obedience to happen.** You might even say that obedience is not really obedience when you're just doing what you want to do and it's just your nature, but when it's hard, that's when you prove your faith—through doing what you should even when you don't want to. Suffering brings out the obedience in us because it gives us a chance to choose not to be angry, bitter, resentful, vengeful, or hateful, even though we naturally want to be. And we aren't because we see pain for what pain is—a lesson in the life of faith.

But sometimes pain is so bad that it threatens to be the death of us. There was a time when Hayley believed that and cowered at its attacks. She feared pain so much that it took all her energy just to fear it, worry about it, and run from it. But once she realized the true value of the death part of pain, she was set free. See, Jesus calls us to a new life in him. We are new creatures, and when that happens the old passes away or dies (see Rom. 6:6–7; 2 Cor. 5:17). And this is a good thing, because the old us is bad, stupid, and lazy. The old us got us into nothing but trouble, and so *dying to that old self* is of great spiritual value. Dying to self is another lesson of pain. When something threatens you with pain, you can say "bring it on" when your goal is not self-preservation but self-destruction—destruction of the old, sinful self. Pain isn't meant to destroy you, but it can destroy the sin in you, so bring it on! Who doesn't want the sin in them taken out?

Suffering and pain also teach you not to hang on so tight to this world but to put all your eggs in the basket of heaven. In Philippians 1:23 Paul talks about how much better things are going to be when we are united with Jesus in heaven. When you suffer here on earth, it should remind you that earth is only temporary and that pain is to be expected, but in heaven it's all done with. Finished. And there things will be so much better than you could ever imagine. You just have to put up with some trials while you are here. But don't worry—this will be over in the blink of an eye (see Rom. 8:18–21).

Pain also teaches you about your need for other people. God planned for us not to be islands but to need each other. Remember what he said back in the Garden of Eden: "It is not good for the man to be alone" (Gen. 2:18). We were meant to live in community with one another, and pain makes that a necessity. When you suffer, you need other people to comfort you and help you. While comforting them is part of your service to God, letting them comfort you is part of that same gift. If nobody needs anybody else, then how will we serve one another? So you can think about your pain as a chance to lean on someone else and to give them the ability to use their gift of service on you. Being needed feels good to people, so don't feel bad when on occasion you desperately need God's people to be by your side.

As you start to take a more biblical look at your pain, you might just see that what's inside you that is hating the suffering isn't really self-preservation at all but is something much more despicable. See, if it's true that suffering is meant for your good, and if it's true that if you suffer you are learning more about God and his role in your life, then running from it would be running from God. ***And if you are running from God, who are you running to?***

What you're about to read might sound totally historic and not relevant at all, but in the Bible God talks a lot about these little things called *idols*. They are little gods, really, that take our attention away from the one true God. They are things and even people that we go to for the things we should be going to God for. So idols can be food, shopping, friends, video games, sports, money, popularity, success, comfort, and the list goes on and on. Anything that makes you feel better, tells you what to do, keeps you from doing what God wants you to do, or leads you to sin as you pursue it is an idol. And idols are oftentimes the first things to scream when pain hits, because pain is meant to destroy them, not you. And they don't want to go.

So when you suffer, think about what it is inside you that is screaming. Is it your need for comfort or rest? Is it your need for protection or respect? The scream needs to be detected and identified as something not to be listened to. One of the valuable things about dying to self is that this process kills our idols. And if you have any understanding of God's Word, then you probably know that idols need to be killed—and not just when you get around to it but right now, because idols keep you away from God and his promises (see 1 Cor. 6:9–10). If you want to be idol-free, then let the pain do its job. So what if it hurts a little? It's worth it if it helps you learn to say, "No, I'm not listening to you anymore, idol. Today I'm turning my thoughts over to God, so scream all you want—la, la, la, la, I can't hear you anymore!"

As a believer you don't want anything or anyone to replace God in your life. You don't want anything to come between you. You love him and you are devoted to him, so when pain comes, accept it as a hot fire that burns away the impurities from your life. Sure, it's hot and it hurts, but if that's what it takes to purify you, then

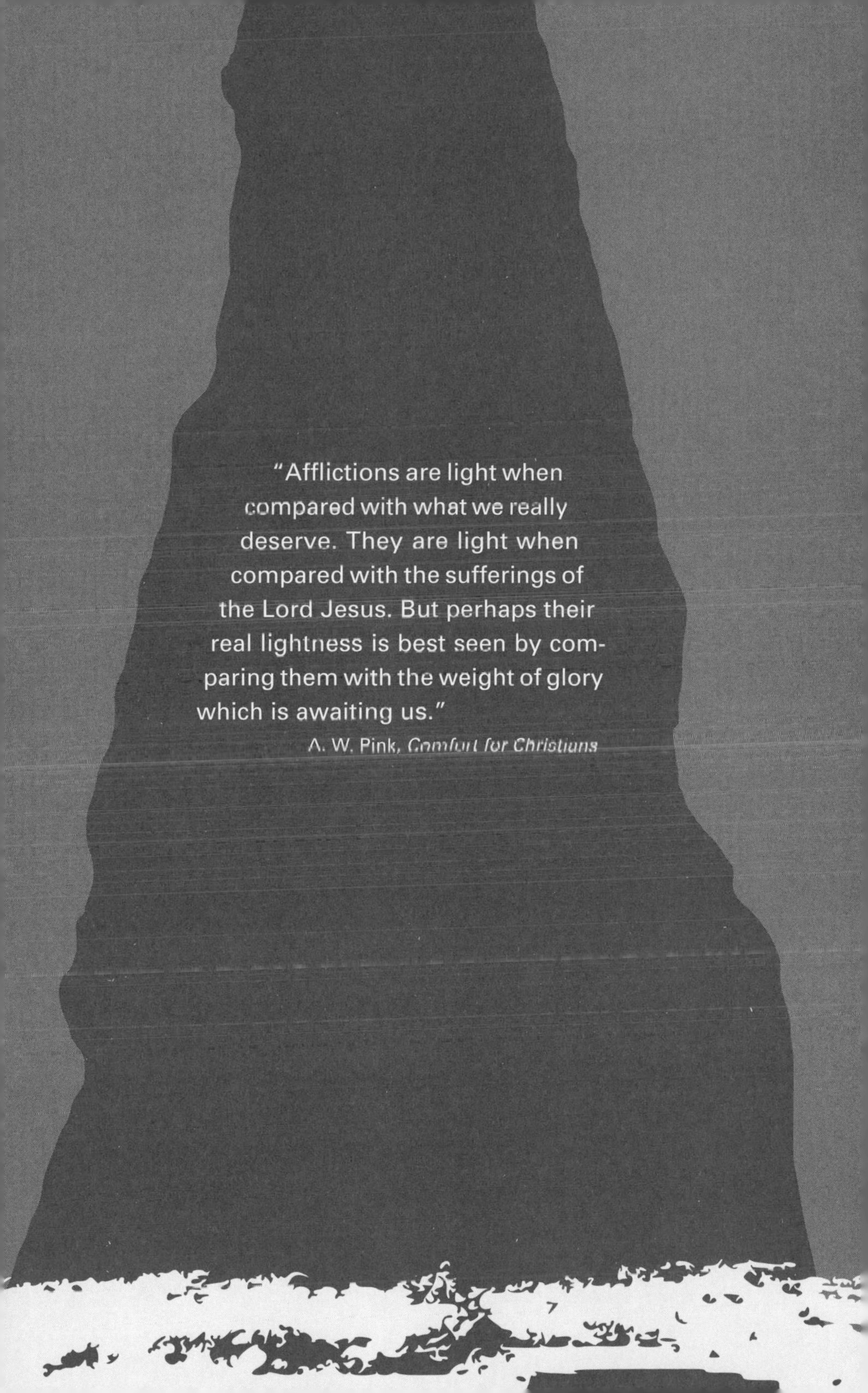

"Afflictions are light when compared with what we really deserve. They are light when compared with the sufferings of the Lord Jesus. But perhaps their real lightness is best seen by comparing them with the weight of glory which is awaiting us."

A. W. Pink, *Comfort for Christians*

why freak out about it? Think about it like this: If you could suffer in order that God might be glorified, wouldn't you do it? Well, then suffer and know that all your suffering *is* ultimately for God's glory.

Jesus gave an example of this when he answered a question about a blind man. His disciples were wondering if the guy was blind because he did something wrong. But Jesus's answer confirmed that it wasn't about what the guy or what his parents did or didn't do, but "he was born blind so that God could show what he can do for him" (John 9:3), which Jesus then proceeded to do by healing the man's blindness. When God can show what he does for us, that brings him the glory.

When God intends something like pain for your good, you can be sure that the heart that trusts him will find good coming its way. Your pain might not end immediately; it might linger for a really long time, but the blessing that comes with it will far overshadow it if you will just trust God and refuse to take matters into your own hands. Let pain do its work, and trust that God will work all things out for your good. For the believer, pain is never the end in itself, or else how could God command us to find joy in it? That's what he does, you know. Check out James 1:2–4:

> Dear brothers and sisters, when troubles come your way, consider it an opportunity for great joy. For you know that when your faith is tested, your endurance

> has a chance to grow. So let it grow, for when your endurance is fully developed, you will be perfect and complete, needing nothing. (NLT)

Trials and pain, suffering and hard times are really a gift from God. After all, they lead to really good stuff—endurance and being perfected. Think about the most amazing and interesting people in the world. Would you say that most of them were people who struggled, suffered, and overcame? Or people who never had a care in the world and had everything handed to them on a silver platter? History confirms it: suffering builds character, it builds story, and it builds a really amazing life. So don't waste your pain, but find the purpose in it and get over it today.

"We know that all things work together for the

good of those who love God—those whom he has called according to his plan."

—ROMANS 8:28

Chapter 4

OVER THE

FAILURE

"Most Bible characters met with ***failure*** and survived. Even when the failure was immense, those who [rebounded] **REFUSED** to lie in the dust and ***bemoan*** their tragedy. In fact, their failure and repentance led to a greater conception of God's **GRACE**. They came to know the God of the second chance, and sometimes the third and fourth."

Oswald Sanders, *Spiritual Leadership*

Fear of Failure

Winning is the best feeling. Losing is the worst. No one wakes up in the morning and says, "I hope I lose today." That's just crazy. Everybody everywhere loves to win. Winning means you're the best, the strongest, the winner. It means you are special—more special than those other losers! And so we all want to win because being a loser is unimpressive and even embarrassing. Our failures are humiliating, for the most part, and that's why we fear failure. The fear of failure can keep you from doing all kinds of things and from even trying, because failure just hurts too much. It's like you can't get over even the thought of failing, so you don't even try.

But failure isn't as bad as all that. In fact, in the life of faith, failure is foundational. After all, it was your failure that led you to the cross. If you hadn't failed, then you wouldn't have needed him. So hooray for failure! It led you to salvation. See, failure, when looked at in the right light, is actually a stepping-stone toward success. In fact, faith without failure is a charade. Where there are imperfect humans, there will inevitably be failure. For the believer, weakness and failure are meant to be not feared but embraced (see 2 Cor. 12:9).

It's a topsy-turvy world we live in where self-esteem, self-confidence, and self-promotion are the normal, healthy choice, thinking low enough of yourself to confess your need for a Savior is weak, and walking humbly is unsafe and even ridiculous. In this world where winning is everything and weakness is to be feared, it's no wonder that we can't get over our failure and accept our inability to do life on our own and our need for God. But what looks like failure and weakness to the naked eye might just be success and strength in the spiritual realm. See, when you are totally independent, successful, and strong, what need do you have for a Savior? Why would you look for God to guide you, to help you, or to comfort you when you've got that all covered your own strong self?

We have a relative who thinks like this. He's so rich that he can do anything and buy anything he wants, and so in response to the gospel he says, "Why do I need God when I can buy anything I want?" His success makes it hard for him to kneel before the throne, and your success can do the same to you. It makes it tough to devote your time to God and to learning what pleases him and what he wants from you. But failure reminds you of your real need for him by bringing you to the place of

"But he told me: 'My kindness is all you need. My power is strongest when you are weak.' So I will brag even more about my weaknesses in order that Christ's power will live in me. Therefore, I accept weakness, mistreatment, hardship, persecution, and difficulties suffered for Christ. It's clear that when I'm weak, I'm strong."

2 Corinthians 12:9–10

knowing that you are in no way big enough, wise enough, or smart enough to do this thing called life on your own. So yippee for failure and for weakness! As the apostle Paul says, "If I must brag, I will brag about the things that show how weak I am" (2 Cor. 11:30).

But getting all happy over your failure isn't a natural or an easy thing. In fact, it's a painful and disgusting thing for the most part. But in the process of learning to get over it, taking a look at your failure and the way you think about it is foundational to your holiness. It's like this: without an accurate understanding of who you really are and why you need a Savior, you won't be drawn to his righteousness, you won't salivate for his presence, and you won't dream of his perfecting humility. Accepting your own weakness so that he can be your strength will not only help you to get over your failure but set you free from the bondage to this world and let the power of heaven loose in your life.

The Humiliation of Failure

Let's face it: it's humiliating to fail. From tripping over one of those invisible cracks in the sidewalk in front of a few strangers to missing a game-winning free throw in front of hundreds of (former) fans, failure makes you feel and look bad. But all is not lost. Nope, the power of failure for the believer is actually found in the humiliation that comes from it. For the believer, the act of being humiliated is really just about finding the ability to look at your life from God's perspective and not your own. Humility is the opposite of pride. And while humility is the foundation of all righteousness, pride is the root of all sin. Pride says, "I can do it on my own. I don't need God. I am important. I am more necessary than you can imagine—even irreplaceable." Pride leads angels to challenge God to a duel. It leads humans to want to have thousands of online friends, followers, and fans. And it keeps you from getting over the stuff in your life that you need to get over.

But humility is the opposite of pride and sets you free to worship the Creator instead of his creation. In humility you find strength in your weakness and hope in your failure. For the humble, the way up is the way down and the way down is the way up. Jesus puts it this way: "Those who honor themselves will be humbled, but people who humble themselves will be honored" (Luke 14:11). It's a spiritual fact of life that makes no sense to the nonspiritual: being last makes you first with God, and insisting on being first puts you last—or haven't you heard it said, "The last will be first, and the first will be last" (Matt. 20:16)? It's not that you should make it your goal to lose or to suffer—that's not it at all—but that you should

Self-Pity Is Pride

Here's the deal: self-pity, self-hate, self-loathing—all of those things that might really look like total humility—are actually pride in disguise. The reason is revealed in the first word in each of them: "self." They are all about self. And whether your occupation with self is with your worthlessness or your worthiness, it's all the same: sinful. We are never to be obsessed with ourselves but are to be obsessed with our God.

know that pride, honoring yourself, and putting yourself before other people denies the life of Christ in you. But putting yourself after others and thinking less highly of yourself immediately identifies you with Christ.

If this all seems too unnatural and complicated, you're right, it is. But while it's unnatural to your flesh, it's natural to your spirit, and while it's complicated to your pride, it's simple for your humility. Fact is, your failure is God's training ground for humility. It goes like this: When you fail you show your weakness, and showing your weakness makes your pride freak. Your pride wants to impress; it wants the applause of people and the glory of feeling good about yourself. But God wants to strip off all that binds you to this world. He wants your eyes on him and your heart open and ready to act when he commands. The only thing keeping you from the powerful life of faith is your pride, and so when your pride gets bruised, hurt, or even sliced up, why do you worry?

Learn to think about failure differently. Think about it like a good workout. Sure, it hurts, but the pain means your muscles are growing. Or think about it like a potter molding a big, gooey pile of clay into a useful vessel. He pounds it into a ball, then throws it down on his wheel and starts the wheel spinning. Then he squeezes and yanks the clay, pushes it down and lifts it up—all this effort and strain just to make a complete, unbroken, useful vessel for himself. Each time you fail, you are being shaped, molded, and made better. And holding on to your pride as if it's a part of you that you can't bear to part with hurts you more than it helps you.

There was a time when Hayley hated to be wrong or to mess up. She was obsessed with knowing it all and being it all. Her nature was to be the star, the center of attention, and she loved it. But when she met her match in Michael, the world started to fall apart. She started having her mistakes and failures pointed out, and it hurt like salt on an open wound. She hated it. At first she argued a lot, trying to prove that she was right and he was wrong. She refused to say she was sorry when she hurt him or messed up. After all, when she was wrong it was just an accident and nothing to apologize for. So she went on in her prideful certainty that she never did anything wrong and everyone else knew nothing. But when she finally came to a point where she saw her own sinfulness in the mirror—when she stopped fighting for herself and started living for truth—an amazing change happened. Suddenly all the fighting, anger, frustration, bitterness, depression, and stress she'd been living with was gone. When she decided to stop fighting for herself and to start living for God, she was set free.

In this case failure was Hayley's doorway to peace, to hope, and to faith. By not continuing to fight off humiliation but letting it do its work, she was able to let it all mean something good and not something destructive. Failure in the eyes of others or even in your own eyes hurts, but it is not the end of the world. It might just be the beginning of something amazing! If you have failure in your life or weaknesses that seem to be your downfall, take heart—you can get over it and get on to a life that can't be destroyed or shaken by anything this world could throw at you. Your failure is about to become your success, so let's get this show on the road.

The Purpose of Failure

We talked about the purpose of pain in chapter 3, and failure, being a lot like pain and sometimes actually leading to pain, has a purpose as well. While a lot of the same stuff that applies to pain applies to failure, there is something more, something amazing that can come when life is no longer about you but about the One who made you. The *Tyndale Bible Dictionary* defines humility as "an ungrudging and unhypocritical acknowledgment of absolute dependence upon God." As we've said, humility is what first brought you to your knees. It was your realization that you needed God because you couldn't do this life without him. And so humility is the foundation of it all. But what do you really know about humility? And how do you handle it when it comes in the form of humiliation from your failures and your weaknesses? How you answer that will determine how well you will get over the bad stuff in your life.

When you fail, you feel like every ounce of pride in you has been scorched with a hot iron, and it makes you recoil in an effort to protect yourself. Your heart races, your blood rushes to your skin, you blush, you get sweaty palms, you feel sick to your stomach—death can seem like a better option! And all you want to do is run and hide in order to make it stop. This sensation of humiliation is painful because it is attacking the part of you that needs acceptance and adoration in order to survive. **Humiliation hurts the part of you that counts on something other than God to be its hope and its salvation.** It hurts your pride and can damage the things that you rely on to make you feel like a unique, special, important, and valuable individual in the eyes of the world. But while all of these things may sound really good, when they don't have their foundation in the One who made you, they are a barrier between you and your Savior. When you find your worth in anything other than who you are as a child of God, eventually you are going to be humbled, you are going to suffer, and you are going to hurt. Sure, you'll suffer and hurt when your worth is all wrapped up in him too, but your suffering and hurt will be of such great value that you will feel no need to complain or worry—you will only count it as essential to your faith.

See, the problem comes because pride puts you at the center of it all. **Pride makes life all about you, when it really isn't all about you at all.** And that opens you up for pain and anguish by perpetuating the myth that your life ought to be this way or that. Pride says things like "I deserve this or that," "I'm better than him," "But she started it," or "He had no right to say that to me." Pride is all about your rights and position compared to other people and never about your position in relation to God. It majors on complaint and offense, as if you were some kind of little god that needs to be honored and worshiped. Pride is ultimately at the root of every problem you have, and it can only be overcome with

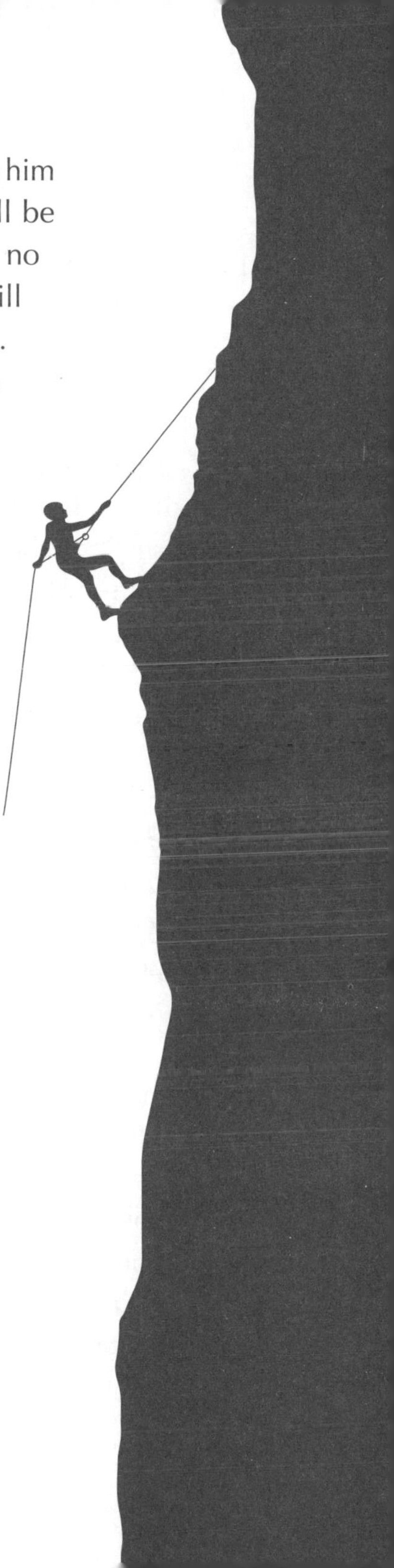

humility. As you start to understand that humility, as commanded by God's Word, has to do with putting up with injury and offense with patient endurance and without bitterness or resentment, you start to see areas in your life where pride, acting in complete rejection of this truth, rears its ugly head.

When you fail and turn to humility instead of pride, you are able to put up with it all. None of it can destroy you or depress you because you're trusting God with all of it. Humility puts all the pain and suffering, failure and weakness into God's hands and trusts him to deal with it. Jesus, our perfect example of a humble human being, lived his life this way. First Peter 2:23 says about him that even in his weakest moment, while hanging on a cross for all to mock, "he didn't make any threats but left everything to the one who judges fairly." See what he did? He could have been prideful and arrogant, but he wasn't; he was meek and humble. And he is the one we are to model ourselves after. The goal of all believers is to become more like Christ (see 1 Cor. 11:1). Humility is the opposite of self-assertiveness and self-interest, and that means that if you were to act in humility in the midst of your failure, you would no longer feel the urge to crawl away and hide in order to protect your image. You would no longer need to do all you could to prove to yourself and everyone watching that you weren't a failure, and you would be set free to let your weakness become your strength.

And that's how it happens—in the hands of a powerful and loving God, all your failure and weakness become your sanctification, your progressive movement toward holiness. Nothing ever slows you down or pushes you back, but instead your soul advances in every circumstance toward the goal of becoming more like Christ. After all, if it was good for Jesus to experience weakness and failure in the eyes of the world, why wouldn't it be just as good for you? Hebrews 5:8 says that his suffering taught him obedience. So how could your failure, your weakness, and the suffering that comes from it not also teach you obedience?

Pride and Failure

If you have trouble getting over your failure, living with your weakness, or handling criticism, then this might come as a shock, but your pride is getting in the way of your happiness. Before you freak out and throw this book on the floor, just let us remind you that pride is something we all struggle with. It's the source of all sin, right? And since we all sin, no exceptions, we can say that we all struggle with pride; we just struggle with it in different areas. We aren't trying to condemn you or call you an arrogant jerk. Our goal is to show you the pride

"Pride cannot trust God. The posture of trust is too weak. Too dependent. It calls too much attention to the strength and wisdom of another. Trusting God is the heartbeat of humility, the opposite of pride."

John Piper, sermon,
"Are You Humble Enough to Be Care-Free?"

in your life so you can kick it and get on with the good life. Because anywhere you can find pride and kill it, you accept your failure to be perfect and make huge strides toward the life of grace, faith, hope, and love.

So let's just take a quick look at some of the ways getting over your pride might actually be the ticket to getting over your failures. No one is looking or listening, so be brutally honest with yourself as you read them. That's the only way to break the habit of pride and get through to the grace of humility.

We've already talked a bit about self-pity, but let's just say again real quick that it's a sign of pride because it's all about how you feel, and how horrible your life is, and how ugly you are, and how bad you did . . . and as you can see, it's all about you! You see, pride doesn't stop and think about God and what he wants for you but thinks only about you and what you want for you (see 1 Cor. 13:5). So self-pity is really another way of criticizing God for your lousy life, and it's the easiest way to not get over things!

Indulging in the luxury of misery, or self-pity, is kind of a cultural norm. We all say things like "I just can't get over it" or "I'm a total failure," and we convince ourselves that we are a particularly hard case, removed from the loving hands of God. But that is a lie. Failure can serve a great purpose in the lives of those who take God at his word. Failure can serve as a reminder that God is in control, not us. It can bring you to your knees and put the unessential things of this world into a better perspective. Fearing failure, or what failure says about you, shows an arrogant belief that who you are is defined by what you do rather than what God has done for you. But there is freedom from the fear of failure when you put your hope and your worth in the one who is worthy.

Another thing about pride that makes failure so unbearable is our need to complain. Do you complain a lot? "I should have won," "I'll never get things right," "I'm sick of being a loser." While your complaining might be focused on your failure, it is really backhanded blame of God himself. Sure, it's not what you're thinking when you're complaining, but complaining is really saying, "I deserve more than this" and "Where is God when I need him?" Really? Do you really deserve more than the eternal life that God gave you absolutely free? Do you really deserve more than the complete and total salvation that can never be taken away from you and assures that you will spend eternity with the most amazing being of all? Has your holiness really been so great that your life should be better than it is right now? Or has your sin been so deceitful that you deserve worse than any other human who has ever lived? Complaint is a sign of who you think you are and what you think about God and his gifts. Your

"What does it matter if external circumstances are hard? Why should they not be! If we give way to self-pity and indulge in the luxury of misery, we banish God's riches from our own lives and hinder others from entering into His provision."

Oswald Chambers,
My Utmost for His Highest

failure as a human being can't be blamed on God through your anger or complaint. All your actions have consequences, and the quickest way to get over the outcome of failure is to stop complaining and start praising God. Stop the complaint and break through to contentment!

A lack of thankfulness is another way that pride keeps you from getting over your failure. Everything good in your life comes from God (see James 1:17), and being unthankful is making the dangerous assumption that you got whatever you have, success or failure, on your own. It's so not true! God decides if it's gonna rain or shine and if you are going to make it or break it. Ultimately he's the giver of all that is good in your life. Proverbs 20:24 says, "The Lord is the one who directs a person's steps. How then can anyone understand his own way?" Knowing this can help you with your failures in life because you can't be depressed when you are thanking God. You can't hate your life when you are thankful for your life. And failure will be seen not as the end but as the beginning when thanking God, even for the bad stuff in life, is your practice.

We hope none of this hurts too much, but if it does, don't freak, because not being able to take criticism is another form of pride (and we don't want to be responsible for you getting your pride on). Criticism is one of two things: either it's the truth and there is some area in your life where you've messed up, or it's wrong and the critical person is making up stuff. Either way, it can hurt. And while hurt might be your first reaction, if you are smart you won't let it linger. If the criticism is wrong, then you have to trust God to fight for you. Trust him to answer for you, to be powerful enough to speak to other people, even critical ones. And if the criticism is true, then thank God that he can use another human being to help get you back on track by pointing out something you might not have seen that might make failure less of a possibility in the future. Wisdom allows criticism to be used by the hand of God to shape you and polish you into the image of Christ (see Prov. 9:8; 15:31; 27:5). We've never met a truly humble person who said, "Man, I can't get any more humble!" Living in humility means that you don't waste anything on useless pain and suffering, but you let it all mean something so it can bring glory to God! When you think like this, failure and the criticism of that failure can't damage you but will only make you stronger.

Let's face it: no one is perfect. We are all gonna fail, but the perfectionist has a hard time coping with that fact. So if perfectionism is your tendency, then listen up, because your need to be perfect is messing with your ability to get over it. You wanna be good, you wanna do what is right, but making "being good" or perfect your god or something you need in order to be acceptable to

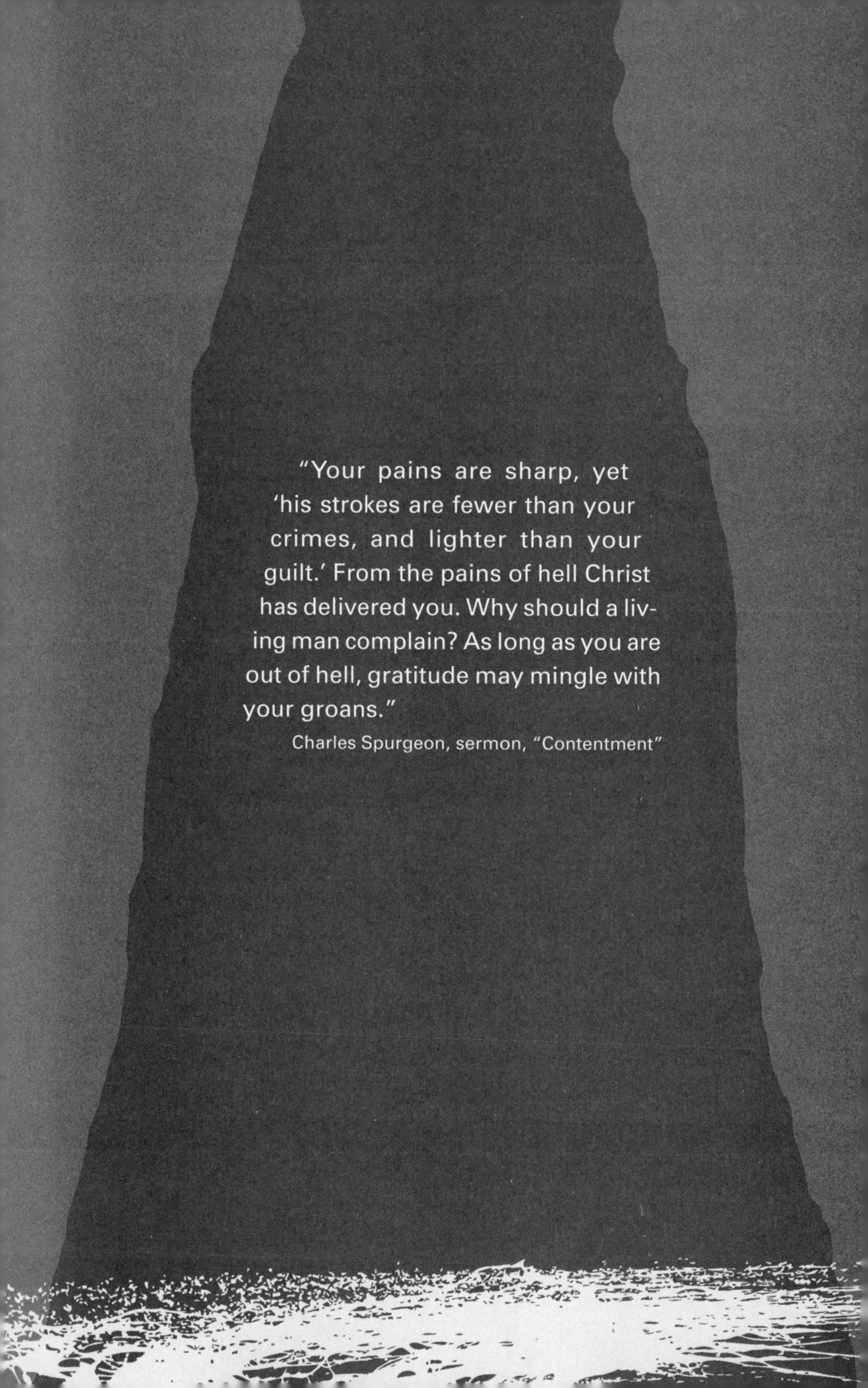

"Your pains are sharp, yet 'his strokes are fewer than your crimes, and lighter than your guilt.' From the pains of hell Christ has delivered you. Why should a living man complain? As long as you are out of hell, gratitude may mingle with your groans."

Charles Spurgeon, sermon, "Contentment"

God is a lie—and not only a lie but a sin. There is *nothing* you need to do to get God's love. You accepted it from him the moment you made Jesus Lord of your life. If perfectionism could save you, then all we'd need would be the Old Testament law, and Christ would have died for nothing. And we all know that ain't true. Galatians 2:21 confirms this with these words: "If we receive God's approval by obeying laws, then Christ's death was pointless." So, yep, you're gonna mess up. You're gonna fail. You're not gonna live up to other people's standards or your own, let alone God's perfect standard, but that's okay, because God wiped out your sin, your failures, your imperfections by the blood of his perfect Son. When you can see the pride in your perfectionism—or the thought that you, unlike every other human being on earth, ought to be without fault or failure—you can see it for how ugly it truly is. The world would have you believe that perfectionism is just another acceptable personality trait, when in reality it is a sin of pride. When you refuse to make sin an acceptable part of your personality, you step away from the fear of failure and the inability to get over it when you do fail.

But sometimes it's not so much your failure you can't get over but someone else's success. If what you are hung up on is not just that you failed but that someone else didn't, your real problem is jealousy. And jealousy is a sign of pride. Again, it's all about you and what you deserve that they have or they took from you. It makes you out to be the one who should be honored, and it also smacks of unthankfulness and resentment toward God. Remember, God is sovereign, meaning nothing gets away from him. If you've failed at doing or getting something you want, you can still know that you only have what God wants you to have (see Exod. 20:17; Col. 3:5). And why would you want more than God has determined is best for you?

On another note entirely, kindness is good. Caring about people, good. Doing good, good. But being a people pleaser is bad because it means you need the approval of others to feel good about yourself. In fact, without their approval you can become a total mess, as if their approval proves your worth. Getting over this kind of obsession has to do with priorities. When people pleasing is your number one goal, then you are going to fail more than you succeed. You weren't meant to please everyone; you were meant to please God! He's the judge of your life, not them. So in order to get over your people-pleasing tendencies, you have to see what Paul nails right here in Galatians 1:10 when he says, "Am I saying this now to win the approval of people or God? Am I trying to please people? If I were still trying to please people, I would not be Christ's servant." Doing what is right or good (or even bad) in order to get the approval, love, or

"Pride must die in you, or nothing of heaven can live in you."

Andrew Murray, *Humility*

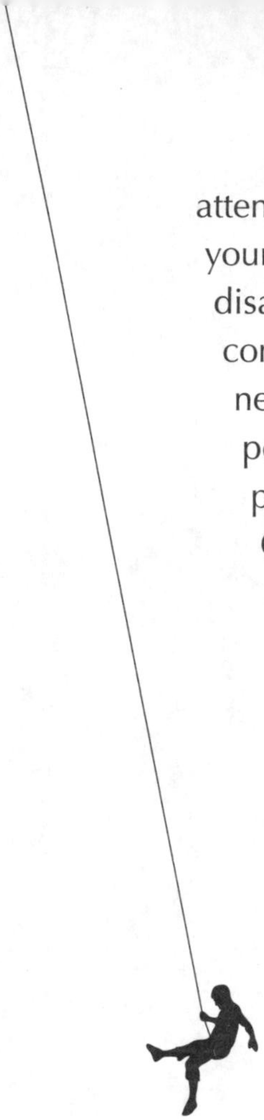

attention of a human being can quickly make your life a mess. You should feel no guilt from disappointing someone; guilt should only come from your sin, and that sin has forgiveness in Christ. So in order to get over your people-pleasing ways, you have to give people less power to judge than you give God. Let go of pleasing them and look to please God, and the people who love God will be well pleased, as will God.

One of the most obvious things pride does in a person is make them think better of themselves than they think of others. This might not sound like it has anything to do with getting over failure, but let us see if we can't change your mind. Think about the person who thinks they are the best singer ever or who thinks that their sin isn't as bad as everyone else's. When people think like this, failure can come as a terrible blow. It cracks their perfect image of self and threatens to destroy who they are. But failure shouldn't surprise us. Truth is, the more you get to know God and his Word, the more you realize how horribly sinful you are. Take a look at the words that Paul wrote. Early on in his faith he called himself the least of the *apostles* (see 1 Cor.

15:9), but over time he started to view himself as the worst of all *sinners* (see 1 Tim. 1:15–16). The closer he got to God, the more he saw himself as sinful, not holy. Paul discovered in his growth as a believer that pride deceives you and keeps you from taking a sober look at the sin in your life that has to go, and it convinces you that failure is unnatural and something to be avoided at all costs. But failure isn't the end but is confirmation that what God says about humanity is right (see Rom. 3:10–12). This should encourage you.

Pride can also show up in the form of impatience with failure. Becoming impatient with your own failure or the failure of others can lead to anger, resentment, and even bitterness. Failure slows down life; it gets in the way of your goals and plans, and the last thing you want to do is to be patient. But patience is a fruit of the Spirit (see Gal. 5:22–23), and its opposite is pride because pride makes your pace, your needs, your wants more important than everyone else's, including God's. If you don't know what to work on next in your spiritual life, try praying that you may become more patient. And just watch what God has you tackle in your life!

A lot of times people can't get over failure because they refuse to even admit failure happened. In this case failure is something so unthinkable and inconsistent with their idea of what it means to be successful that they refuse to even see the truth that failure happens. No one is perfect; everyone messes up, and pretending you won't only sets you up for a major bummer once you do mess up. Pride and the inability to admit failure are about covering up sin and pretending to be what you aren't. The opposite of that is transparency, and in the life of a believer it's crucial. Pretending we've got it all under control is what makes people call Christians hypocrites. Acting like you never make a mistake or have it all together is a total lie, and trying to keep up that image can break you.

Here's another symptom of pride: fear of admitting you were wrong or of saying "I'm sorry." If you can't say "I was wrong," then pride is in the house. People who can't say they are sorry have a huge fear of failure because it leaves them feeling vulnerable, exposed. Saying you're sorry really hurts the pride; it means you were, well, wrong, and for the prideful person, being wrong is unacceptable. Failure becomes less of an obstacle when you can swallow your pride and say you're sorry.

And last but not least, consider the pride of isolation and its power to keep you from getting over your failure. When you fail in a really big way, the easiest thing to do is to disappear. You want to hide out so no one will see you, and that's just what the enemy would have you do. See, isolation is the opposite of community. And God created us for community. In community we pray for one

"A stiff apology is
a second insult."
G. K. Chesterton

another, we bear one another's burdens, and we love one another. In isolation the battle is a lonely and exhausting one. Failure holds on for dear life in the person who is alone, but being brave enough to walk into the community of believers and to accept the acceptance of others, even for your failure, often brings just the healing that is needed after failure. A lot of failure can be healed, or gotten over, in community in two different ways. Check out these verses and see how you can find healing where there are other believers:

> So admit your sins to each other, and pray for each other so that you will be healed. (James 5:16)

> Help carry each other's burdens. In this way you will follow Christ's teachings. (Gal. 6:2)

Sin likes darkness, but bringing our pain, our suffering, and our sin into the light of community can set us free from the painful symptoms that come with failure. If you have sinned, find a healthy community to speak God's forgiveness over you, and if you have a burden, then let someone share it as you share their burdens in turn. When you do, getting over your failure will be a quick work.

> See how good and pleasant it is
> when brothers and sisters live together in harmony! (Ps. 133:1)

Remember, all of this talk about failure and pride is not meant to condemn you but to give you hope. See, those things in your life that you can't get over that come from your failure and your weakness aren't meant to destroy you but to make you stronger. But if you can't spot them, then you can't fix them, and all we want to do is help. It's important you understand that all this is an exercise in grace and not in condemnation. God's grace is offered to everyone, sinners the world over, as a hand up out of the mire and muck.

If you believe that God is unwilling to help you, you are wrong; his Word says, "He will not always accuse us of wrong or be angry with us forever. He has not treated us as we deserve for our sins or paid us back for our wrongs" (Ps. 103:9–10). If you think that you are unworthy of his help, you are wrong; he is merciful: "We were dead because of our failures, but he made us alive together with Christ" (Eph. 2:5). If you've been in this pride rut for a long time, don't freak; his Word says he is "slow to anger" (Num. 14:18 NIV). And if you think you are too bad because your sin is worse than anything anyone else has done, you are wrong; there is no sin he can't forgive, except the sin of not believing in him (see Matt. 12:31–32).

You can get over everything in your life by trusting God and taking him at his word. Even if you're stuck in the pit of weakness, your body is failing, and your mind is faltering—no matter how weak you might feel right now—know that it's okay. In fact, it's better than okay, because God uses the weak things of this world to shame the strong (see 1 Cor. 1:27).

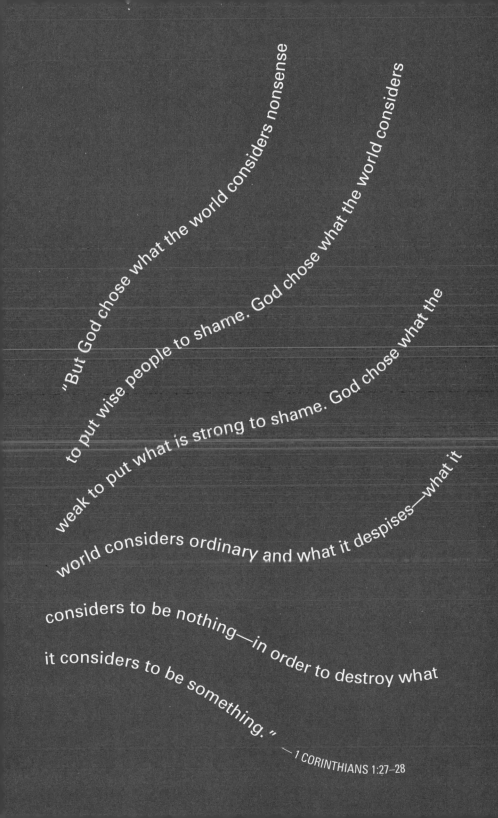

"But God chose what the world considers nonsense to put wise people to shame. God chose what the world considers weak to put what is strong to shame. God chose what the world considers ordinary and what it despises—what it considers to be nothing—in order to destroy what it considers to be something."

—1 CORINTHIANS 1:27–28

Chapter 5

OVER THE

UNFORGIVENESS

"Unforgiveness is like drinking ***poison*** and expecting the one who ***sinned*** against you to **DIE**."

Unknown

Unforgiveness

Getting over guilt, pain, and failure is not a walk in the park. It's more like a fall from the monkey bars! But compared to living with the feeling of unforgiveness, it's all a piece of cake. Unforgiveness is the state you live in when you cannot forgive someone who has hurt you or when you feel like you can't be forgiven for something you've done. And when you live in it, it can become a strong undercurrent in everything you do and say. You might not consciously think about the pain of unforgiveness, but your body holds on to it for dear life, and so it takes all of your energy and taints most of your decisions. Unforgiveness that is lived with for years and years literally shapes who you become. It affects all your relationships and your choices. It shapes you into its image and pulls you away from the image of Christ. After all, Christ's reason for existence here on earth was forgiveness. He himself brought forgiveness for all. And so failing to fully take hold of forgiveness is failure to take hold of Christ himself.

But forgiveness isn't easy and it isn't natural. In fact, the world encourages us to avoid it. We all by nature seem to distrust others' motives; we all assume the worst when people are mean or hurtful. We see them as bad and as unlovable. We resent what they have done to us, and we want some kind of justice to be done. We want the score to be settled, even if we have to do it ourselves. And so we live our lives with thoughts of paying back evil for evil and setting things right. But when it comes to getting forgiveness for our own mistakes, we live with fear and worry, stress and strain over the terrible thing we have done that we think we could never be forgiven of by any human, let alone God.

Why is this? Because inside each of us is this notion that sin requires punishment. When we see something bad happen, we say stuff like "That's not fair" or "Someone needs to do something about that." We know deep within our DNA that wrong deserves discipline, and as fallen human beings we are eager to hand out some of that ourselves. We even want to punish ourselves at times when our own sin seems just too ugly for anyone to forgive. This sense that what we have done is too big even for God's grace isn't an unusual one. Millions of people all over the world are living in this kind of pain, which is such a shame because getting over unforgiveness is actually one of the easiest things a person could ever do, and we're gonna tell you how to do it.

Before we dive in, let's just take a little quiz to see how much we have been able to get over so

"Forgiving costs us our sense of justice. We all have this innate sense deep within our souls, but it has been perverted by our selfish sinful natures. We want to see 'justice' done, but the justice we envision satisfies our own interests. We must realize that justice has been done. God is the only rightful administrator of justice in all of creation, and His justice has been satisfied. In order to forgive our brother, we must be satisfied with God's justice and forego the satisfaction of our own."

Jerry Bridges,
The Practice of Godliness

far, shall we? Answer the questions on page 139 before you read on.

If you answered yes to any of these questions, then you are living with unforgiveness, and it's got to be painful. Unforgiveness left to fester in your heart leads to all kinds of yuck. Stuff like bitterness, anger, resentment, and even depression can come from the fact that someone has done something wrong to you and you can't get over it and forgive them. It eats you from the inside out, and it's not a good way to live. People can do some things that are just plain awful, and it's horrible when they do them to you. But what's even more horrible is living with the pain day in and day out, just like they are hurting you over and over. It's no way to live—and it's not the way God wants you to live.

If you didn't answer yes to any of these, then congrats! That's awesome. But while you don't have to read on, it might just be a good exercise to study forgiveness so you can share it with others around you who struggle with the concept. So let's get going down the path of getting over what people do to other people and what we do to God.

The Symptoms of Unforgiveness

If you took the quiz, then you are probably starting to get the idea that unforgiveness brings with it

Over It?

1. Has something happened in your past that makes you sick when you think about it?
2. Do you feel resentment over something someone has done to you?
3. Do you start to feel bitter when you think about a past experience with someone?
4. Do you have fantasies about getting revenge on someone?
5. Is there someone you wish would get a taste of their own medicine?
6. Is there someone you can't bring yourself to pray for because they have hurt you so badly?
7. Is there someone you just can't forgive for what they've done?
8. Have you done something you think God will never forgive you for?
9. Is there a sin in your life you think disqualifies you from the hope of a better future?

all kinds of terrible little traits that trip you up and make your life miserable. Some of the most obvious symptoms of not being able to get over what someone has done are bitterness, resentment, anger, a desire for revenge, and even depression. They make you a victim of the past action perpetrated against you and of your own unforgiveness. But when you live under the grace of God, this tragedy doesn't have to redefine you. When you can learn to get over the pain and even get through to forgiveness, you can take what has happened to you and turn it into a good thing, another tool in the hand of the potter who is shaping you and building you into a vessel useful for his service, instead of forever remaining a victim of the hands of someone else.

This failure to get over what has been done to you leads to obsessing over it—thinking about it all the time, talking about it nonstop, even dreaming of it. And that stresses you out. It makes you irritable, uneasy, and even sick. It can give you stomachaches, ulcers, heart problems, and all kinds of stress. When your body is under such pressure, you can want to medicate yourself to feel better. You may start down the nasty road of trying to numb the pain by drinking, cutting, doing drugs, having sex—anything you can find to stop the pain brought on not just by the actual experience but also by continually reliving it in your mind. Yep, unforgiveness is a doorway to all kinds of junk.

When forgiveness isn't something you need to give someone else but something that you need to get, things can get just as bad. Living with feelings of guilt, like we talked about in chapter 2, can lead to all kinds of problems, the worst of which is just ending it all. See, our bodies weren't meant to live holding on to such pressure and doling out such judgment. We need to take all our pain and suffering, all our guilt and shame to the cross and leave it there. But refusing to do that a lot of times is the easier choice. We do some pretty bad stuff, and then we think that a holy God could never forgive it. And that kind of agony will taint everything you do and say. It will steal your confidence, dash your hope, and destroy your ability to love anything but the pain that you nurse day in and day out. That's the trouble with unforgiveness: it makes the pain of the offense the most important thing in the world. But we all know God should hold that number one position. So in order to start you on the road to forgiveness, let's take a look first at how forgiveness takes place.

Feeling Unforgivable?

We mentioned earlier that Jesus came to earth with the sole purpose of forgiving us sinful humans. You realize that, right? He gave up his heavenly existence (see Phil. 2:6–8) and became a baby who was born in a stinky, cold, uncomfortable stable. He lived a simple life, not filled with the royal treatment, fine food, and expensive clothes but with nothing but the shirt on his back as he walked from town to town healing the sick and forgiving the repentant. He suffered a horrendous death on the cross, ridiculed and scorned by people who thought they were better than him, all for the purpose of forgiving you for your sins. Why would he put in all that work and go through all that pain and suffering if it wasn't enough to forgive you for your incredibly horrible sins (see Gal. 2:21)? Sounds silly when you put it that way, doesn't it? Not only is it silly, but it's blasphemous to say that Jesus's death and resurrection wasn't enough for you because your sin is a particularly impossible case. But that's what you say when you declare, "God can never forgive me for what I did" or "I can't forgive myself for what I did." Let's take a look at these two statements, shall we?

"God can never forgive me for what I did."

As believers we all fully realize that sin deserves punishment. But where we get it wrong is when we start to grade sins on a scale of 1 to 10, with 1 being little sins and 10 being monster sins that deserve life in prison or the death penalty. As human beings we understand the concept of judgment a whole lot better than the concept of grace. Grace, God's kindness to sinners, makes no sense to us when sins start to clock out at an 8, a 9, or even a 10.

Everyone's sin scale is different, but most would agree that murder, for example, is tipping the scale at a big 1-0. Doesn't get much bigger than that. And child abuse is probably up at the top end of the scale too. Sexual perversion, rape, torture—those have got to be high on everyone's list as well. In fact, this scale is even recognized by the most hardened, unrepentant criminals in the world—prisoners in maximum security prisons have a special hatred for certain sinners. Did you know that they consider child murderers and child abusers to be heinous criminals and single them out for special ridicule and attack? Even these hardened convicts rate sins by how disgusting they are. It's human nature. And it's where our sense of being too sinful for forgiveness comes from.

If the sin you struggle with seems especially high on the scale to you, then accepting God's forgiveness can become almost impossible unless you understand one very important spiritual

"We need not climb up into heaven to see whether our sins are forgiven: let us look into our hearts, and see if we can forgive others. If we can, we need not doubt but God has forgiven us."

Thomas Watson, *Body of Divinity*

concept. And it's this: according to God, all sin is equally bad. All of it. There is no sliding scale. All of it is a prideful turning away from our Creator toward ourselves and our desires. And it all requires the blood of Jesus to cover it up. That's why the girl who disobeys her parents needs just as much forgiveness as the man who tortures Christians for their faith.

God's grace doesn't see degrees of evil; it just sees evil and forgives it all based on one thing: the sacrifice of Jesus.

A good example of this is the life of Paul. Doesn't it seem like he would feel the most sinful and least worthy of forgiveness when he had just stopped torturing Christians? But remember what he said about himself as time went on and he grew closer to God? Early in his faith he called himself the worst of the apostles, then as he got further along in his faith he saw himself as the worst of all sinners (see 1 Cor. 15:9; 1 Tim. 1:15–16). He didn't consider his early violent sin to be worse than his post-salvation sin. In fact, he saw the sin he committed long into his walk of faith as adding up to more horror than his prior sin, not because of the level of sin but because of his level of awareness that all sin is against God. The more you understand the grace of God, the more you realize how much he has forgiven you of. And when you see that, every day is a miracle. Every day you live in his grace is unbelievable. Every sin he forgives is awesome—not just the big ugly ones but the little unseen ones. Even the acceptable ones that other people would never blink an eye at are totally unacceptable to the new you. So know that no sin you could commit could ever separate you from his grace (see Rom. 8:38–39).

No matter what your sin, God's promise is the same: if you confess your sins, he is faithful to forgive them (1 John 1:9). Once you confess your sin, the next step is change or repentance. That just means you decide to stop living in that sin any longer. That doesn't mean you might not occasionally slip up and take the bait of temptation, but it does mean that as soon as you figure out what you did, you stop and confess again right there. You don't say, "Oh well, I'll just do this for now and ask forgiveness later." No, you call a sin a sin and then thank God for his immediate forgiveness. It's that simple. So know that your sin, no matter how ugly, isn't too ugly for the blood of Christ to cover it and make you white as snow (see Isa. 1:18).

"I can't forgive myself for what I did."

But what if what's hard for you isn't believing God but forgiving yourself? What if you just can't stop feeling bad about it, can't get over it, and keep thinking you deserve punishment? Maybe you take that job on yourself and you start to hurt yourself,

The Unforgiveable Sin

There is a sin that is unforgivable. It is what the Bible calls blasphemy against or cursing of the Holy Spirit (see Matt. 12:31–32). The way to know if you have committed it or not is by asking yourself this: Do I care what God thinks of my sin? Do I want his forgiveness? If you do, then you have not committed an unpardonable sin. Those who have could care less if God forgave them or not because they don't care about him.

neglect yourself, or otherwise pay yourself back for your royal mess-up. No matter what, saying that you can't forgive yourself is saying that your standards are higher than God's. Sure, he can forgive you for what you did, but your rules are more strict than his—you've got standards, after all, and you broke 'em.

First of all, let's just clear up one thing: when you sin you don't break anybody's law but God's. If you break your own rules, it's not a sin, because sin is always something done against God. So whose forgiveness do you need—yours or God's? Since the Bible never commands you to "forgive thyself for thy sinful ways," you can stop with the crazy notion that you even need to forgive yourself. Okay? Let that thought be just an error of your youth (or some pop psychologist), and let's get on with wisdom.

The only forgiveness you need is from God, and the only thing you need to do for yourself is to get over it. That means you have to get over thinking you are some kind of special sinner who needs more grace than all the rest of us and get over not trusting God with handling judgment. It's a terrible thing to take something that is God's; he's not cool with that. Vengeance is his (see Rom. 12:19) and so is judgment (see Ps. 75:7), so why are you trying to dole it out on yourself? That's just crazy talk. So getting over the sense that you just can't forgive yourself takes only one thing: you have to stop playing God. No offense, but that's what it is, and it isn't something new—we all do it. Hayley's done it many times; Michael's done it; we all do it. It's part of our sinful nature. We think we've got our lives covered and feel confident that we know what's best for us, and in the case of our most horrible sins, we are sure that something must be done. But something has been done! It was done over two thousand years ago, and nothing you can do can improve upon it. So get over it and get on with God's grace, his free forgiveness for all who ask for it. It's yours for the taking today—all you have to do is take it!

And one more thing: we know that in light of your sin, it can be easy to think that you've messed up too much to ever be used by God. That just isn't true. ***God specializes in using broken and sinful people to further his kingdom.*** Just look at the life of David, who was called a man after God's own heart (see Acts 13:22). He slept with Bathsheba, then killed her husband to cover up the whole thing (see 2 Sam. 11). Look at the life of Paul, who was used to pen much of the New Testament even though he had killed Christians before his conversion. God's

Forgiving God

You might wonder, *Do I have to forgive God first, before I can forgive others?* No. Forgiving God is blasphemy because it says that God has done something that needs to be forgiven, which would mean that God had sinned. Impossible! Unbiblical! No way! God cannot sin, and he does no wrong, so he never needs anyone's forgiveness. Anything that happens to you that is bad is not God doing something that requires forgiveness; it is his hand allowing something in your life that is meant for your good should you choose to let it be. So don't get caught up in the lie that you have to forgive God before you can forgive anybody else!

specialty is using sinful people. So get over the idea that you've messed up worse than a murderer and a persecutor. Even if you have, it's no surprise to God, and your level of sinfulness has nothing to do with his ability to get things done through you.

Unable to Forgive

Okay, we've figured out how to accept the forgiveness of God in your life. Now let's talk about your inability to get over or to forgive someone who has hurt you. Thinking about forgiving the sin that others have done to you can make you sick to your stomach, but as we've talked about already, not forgiving can be even worse. The side effects of unforgiveness are overwhelming, so let's see if we can't help you get over unforgiveness toward others.

When Jesus was on earth, he talked about forgiveness and how important it is. That makes sense, doesn't it? Since he has offered you forgiveness for anything you could ever do, why wouldn't he expect you to do the same? Maybe you've read the story of the worker who was forgiven a huge debt he owed his boss but then went out and immediately threw a guy in jail for the small amount he owed him (see Matt. 18:21–35). Jerk! Who would be forgiven a huge debt and then freak out on someone who owed him five bucks? Since God has forgiven you so much ugly, repeated, selfish, prideful sin, shouldn't you have mercy on other human beings who mess up just like you? Makes sense, right? So let's take a look at a few of the things that God says about forgiveness.

In the book of Matthew, Jesus talks about our forgiveness beyond just confessing and repenting. He says that it requires something of you in relationship to other people—your forgiveness. Check it out: "If you forgive the failures of others, your heavenly Father will also forgive you. But if you don't forgive others, your Father will not forgive your failures" (Matt. 6:14–15; see also Matt. 18:21–35).

So if you can't get over what someone has done to you, then how can you expect God's forgiveness? That one hurts us too. How many times do we condemn other people for their sin while we have ugly sin of our own? How crazy is that? We hate that. But we aren't judging you for doing the same thing we are doing, because we know we're wallowing around in the same swamp. That's our condition—we are all stuck in the same swamp of sin, so judging someone else for their inability to get out of the thick, sticky swamp is ridiculous since you can't get out of it either.

In Colossians the apostle Paul says, "Make allowance for each other's faults, and forgive anyone who offends you. Remember, the Lord forgave you, so you must forgive others" (Col. 3:13 NLT). It couldn't be any more clear: God commands forgiveness. It's

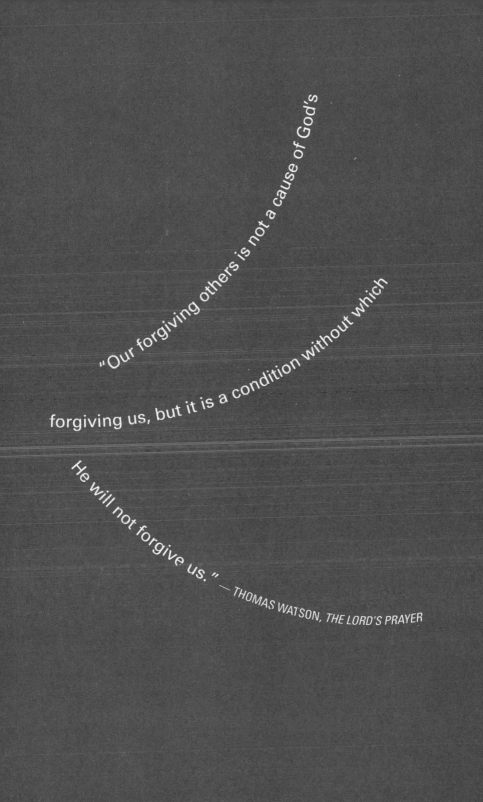

"Our forgiving others is not a cause of God's forgiving us, but it is a condition without which He will not forgive us." —THOMAS WATSON, *THE LORD'S PRAYER*

"Forgiveness is not that stripe which says, 'I will forgive, but not forget.' It is not to bury the hatchet with the handle sticking out of the ground, so you can grasp it the minute you want it."

D. L. Moody

a part of his nature, and he wants it to be a part of ours. But before you freak out and say you just can't do it, let us clear up a few confusing ideas about forgiveness.

First of all, you can forgive someone for their sins, but that doesn't mean that you suddenly forget. And that means that forgiveness doesn't mean suddenly naïvely trusting them not to hurt you yet again; it just means offering them grace and not using their offense against them again. How do you do it? When you forgive someone, you promise not to hold what they did against them, using it as leverage to get them to do what you want or as an excuse to be angry with them. You don't ever throw it in their face or use it as a source of friction between you. When God forgives a sinner of their sin, he doesn't hold their sin against them and keep them from his presence, but he says, "I won't let what you did separate you from me any longer." So you can't hold a grudge after forgiving someone. And that's good, because that means that you can't get all frustrated, bitter, or angry anymore because you've gotten over it. That's a good thing.

The second thing that happens when you forgive someone is that you promise not to tell other people about what they did. You don't complain, share, vent, or anything of the sort unless they could be a danger to others (like an abuser). Other than those cases where the other person is committing crimes against you or others and the authorities need to be involved, you keep your mouth shut because you have forgiven them. To keep talking about it is to prove that you have not forgiven them at all.

And finally, when you forgive someone, you promise not to obsess over it. You don't think about it over and over, imagining how you could have responded or thinking about what they should have done. You don't keep it in your head; you get over it. You've got to, because if you keep thinking about it, you keep convicting them of what they've done, and that's the opposite of forgiveness. The Bible says that God removes our sin from us "as far as the east is from the west" (Ps. 103:12 NIV). That means he doesn't keep thinking about it but puts it out of his mind. So each time what the person did comes into your thoughts, don't freak like you've failed; just say, "No, I'm not gonna think about that anymore." And then change the subject for yourself. That's how forgiveness becomes real.

Peter asked Jesus how many times we should forgive someone—"seven times?" With this Peter thought he was being generous, but Jesus answered, "No, not seven times but seventy times seven!" (see Matt. 18:21–22). The point Jesus made with Peter wasn't to keep count a different way but to always forgive, no matter how many times it's been. Use this to help you to forgive the person again every time you start to want to think about or talk about

Forgiving others means you are loving them the way God loves you. What does love look like in the believer's life? Check it out:

"Love is patient. Love is kind. Love isn't jealous. It doesn't sing its own praises. It isn't arrogant. It isn't rude. It doesn't think about itself. It isn't irritable. It doesn't keep track of wrongs. It isn't happy when injustice is done, but it is happy with the truth. Love never stops being patient, never stops believing, never stops hoping, never gives up" (1 Cor. 13:4–7).

what happened. There is no limit to how many times you need to just get over it.

What Forgiveness Looks Like

Now, with some people forgiveness isn't possible in the sense of literally saying to them, "I forgive you for what you have done to me." And here's why: if someone has sinned but has not confessed the sin or repented from it, then you can't verbally offer them forgiveness. See, God's Word puts a condition on forgiveness for all of us. We get God's forgiveness when we confess our sins to him—remember 1 John 1:9? If God requires confession of us in order to offer us his forgiveness, then why wouldn't we require the same?

So here's how it works. Jesus puts it like this: "If a believer sins, correct him. If he changes the way he thinks and acts, forgive him. Even if he wrongs you seven times in one day and comes back to you seven times and says that he is sorry, forgive him" (Luke 17:3–4). In this, Jesus points out that before forgiveness comes an acknowledgment of sin and a change of action. So forgiving someone who hasn't confessed their sin would be like walking up to some man who slugs you in the face and then laughs about it and saying, "That's okay, I forgive you." He'll just laugh some more. "Forgive me for what? There's nothing to forgive." It won't make any sense to him because in his mind he's done nothing wrong. It's the same in the spiritual realm. God doesn't say "your sins are forgiven" to people who have not confessed their sin and are continuing to live in it. That would mean that sin held no real weight to God, and we know that isn't true.

Here's another example: Many years ago a couple of boys went to school with guns and started shooting people. They killed their friends, and then they killed themselves. A few weeks later a famous pastor who didn't even live in the same state made the statement, "We forgive you boys." Doesn't that sound odd to you? The boys never repented. We don't know if they were sorry for what they did, but chances are they weren't. Besides, those boys didn't kill the pastor or any of his family or friends, so who is he to offer forgiveness for an offense that wasn't even done to him? That would be like us forgiving some girl who is spreading rumors about you to all your friends. Ridiculous!

So if forgiveness isn't something you have to give freely to everyone, then what does that mean about the pain of unforgiveness over offenses where there is no confession? It means that all that is left for you to do is to get over it. You get over it in the same way that you forgive other than saying the words "I forgive you." You don't hold it against them. You don't complain about them to others. And you don't dwell on it. Do those three things and you will be

"Forgiveness is me giving up my right to hurt you for hurting me."

— UNKNOWN

over it even if they are completely unrepentant. People who fail to do these three things keep their identity as "the victim." If you keep thinking about it, it's like they keep doing it to you over and over again. And complaining about it or talking to others about it nonstop requires you to think about it. So in order to get over it, you have to stop reliving the offense. As long as you keep reliving it and making it important in your life, you will never get over it—never.

The final step in getting over it, whether they have confessed and repented or not, is turning it all over to God and trusting him to work everything out for good (see Rom. 8:28). **When God becomes more powerful and more important in your life than the sin that happened to you, then you will finally be set free.**

We've experienced this personally. Every offense that has happened to us, we consider a blessing because we know that it served to move us in the direction God wanted us to go. A few years ago Hayley had a dream come true: a huge speaking tour asked her to speak on it, and it was heaven. But when there was a miscommunication about something, they chose to let Hayley go rather than work through it with her. This was total devastation to Hayley. She didn't see it coming till the day they said good-bye. And while it hurt for quite some time, Hayley had to get over it. So she decided to look at it from the perspective of God's providence and believe that God arranges things, even what seem like disasters, to move us to where he wants us to be next. As Michael often points out, it was right after Hayley getting let go that we got pregnant with our one and only daughter. And that probably wouldn't have happened if Hayley was still busy traveling on tour. Now there is no question that being let go from that tour was the best thing that ever happened in her life! It just took getting over it to realize that. God honors your efforts to get over it and your trust in his providence. He has everything under control!

It has been said that because we are the most forgiven people in the world, we should be the most forgiving people in the world. Do you see it? If you want to get over the unforgiveness in your life, then you've got to take God at his word. You've got to trust him more than you trust your pain or your anger. Feelings are really good at lying. They can get you all worked up over something that God wants you to just drop, and they can convince you that something ungodly needs to be done about them. So don't let your feelings define your faith, but be wise and look into God's Word for the truth that you need to survive the pains of the sin in you and the sin around you.

Your forgiveness was secured the day Jesus came to this earth, and the forgiveness you give to others is a sign of your faith in that forgiveness (see Luke 7:47). Don't deny God's Word by failing to get over the sins of others. Remember what is at stake: "For if you forgive others their trespasses, your heavenly Father will also forgive you, but if you do not forgive others their trespasses, neither will your Father forgive your trespasses" (Matt. 6:14–15 ESV). Make your forgiveness complete by vowing to forgive others who confess their sins and getting over those who don't.

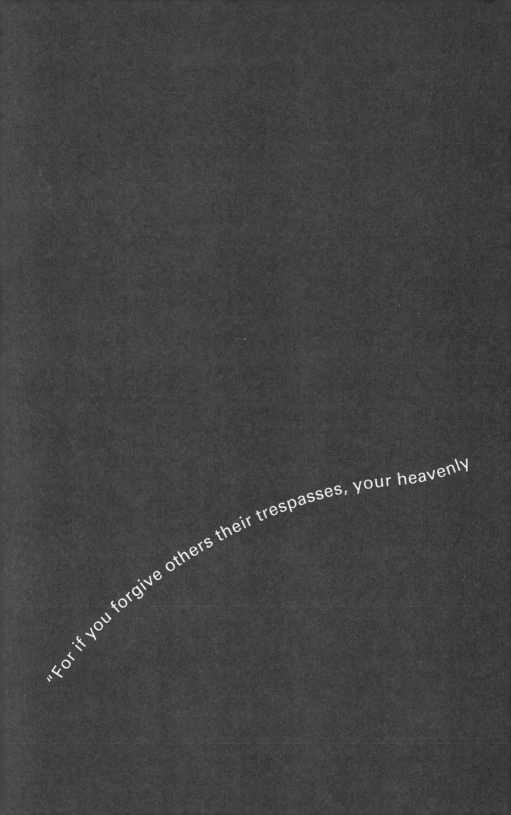

"For if you forgive others their trespasses, your heavenly

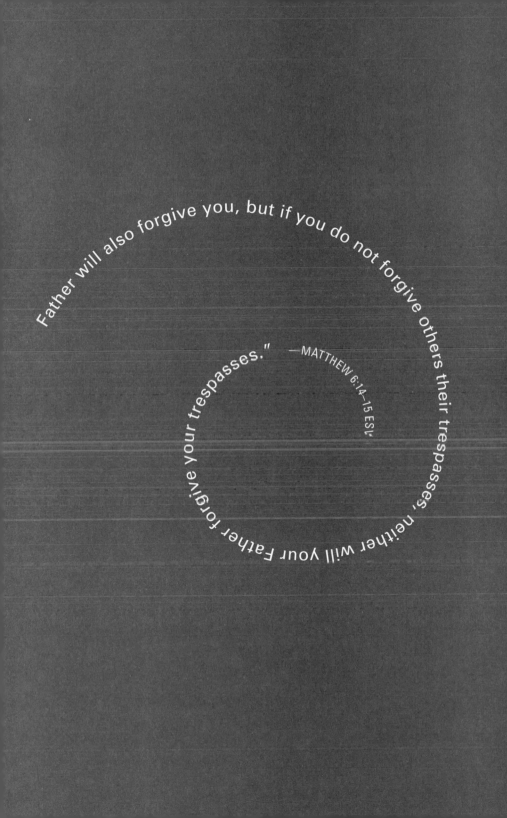

Father will also forgive you, but if you do not forgive others their trespasses, neither will your Father forgive your trespasses." —MATTHEW 6:14–15 ESV

Chapter 6

FINALLY

OVER IT

"Much ***sickness***—physical, mental, and emotional—surely must come from ***disobedience***. Sometimes the patient knows well what his trouble is and for this very reason has not consulted the Lord, ***fearing*** what He will say: **CONFESS**. Turn around. Quit that indulgence. Do not pity yourself. ***Forgive*** that person. Pay back what you owe. Apologize. Tell the truth. Deny ***yourself***. Consider the other's well-being. Lay down your **LIFE**."

Elisabeth Elliot, *The Glad Surrender*

The Past Doesn't Equal the Future

You can't change the past. It can't be done. But you can make the past mean something. You can apply God's Word to your sin and the sin in the lives of those around you and allow it to become a balm for your pain, worry, weakness, and guilt.

If you want to be finally, truly over it, consider your sin and how you can avoid it in the future: Why did you do what you did? What did you think the payoff would be? What were you looking for that you thought you had to have? What does your answer say about what you value? How do your values in that situation differ from God's? What have you been guilty of worshiping in the past? How can you destroy that idol and make a change in your life?

You can't let the mistakes of the past define your future. You must look at them in the light of truth and refuse to be a victim to your choices and your spiritual weaknesses a moment longer. You can take control of your life today by getting over your past. When you determine that you must get over your past so that it can't destroy you, you allow your memories, sins, and pain to be redeemed and used for good. The choice is entirely yours. No one else can set you free from the prison you have put around yourself. God is offering you the key, but he won't open the doors for you. You must be willing to open them and to walk through to redemption.

How disgusting is it when a dog throws up all of his partially chewed kibbles and then a few minutes later, while it's still steamy warm, comes back and licks it all up? Disgusting! But when you refuse to get over it, you are just like that dog. This is a biblical truth explained in Proverbs 26:11, and it still applies today. Don't go back to the thrown-up pile of partially chewed sin from your past and rechew it. It has no value to you and only brings the same sickness back into your life that you threw up. Gross!

Using the Past for Good

When it comes to your past, what's the use? How can the things you've done or that have been done to you be of significant value rather than bringing destruction? That's a question you really need to think about. If God's Word is true, then it's true all the time and in every verse. And if his Word promises that all sin can be redeemed (see Mark 3:28; Rom. 3:23–24) and that all things can work together for the good of those who love him (see Rom. 8:28), then you have to know that is true, even for you.

The only bad memory is one that isn't used for your good. Anything that has ever happened to you can benefit you when you look at it in the light of God's decision to allow it to take place for your benefit. Remember, he is all good. If God allows a thing to happen, then find the reason why. Figure out what spiritual benefit he plans for it to bring you. Don't be a dummy and let the past destroy you instead of making you stronger. There are no bad memories except those that aren't redeemed. God allows or doesn't allow trouble in your life for a reason. Look at the life of Job: Satan couldn't touch him without God first giving him permission (see Job 1–2).

If you want to put your past to work, allowing it to be used for good and not bad, then here's what you can do: Make a list of the things that you just can't seem to get over. Write them all out on a sheet of paper. Then after each one write what lesson God might want to teach you. If you aren't sure, do some research.

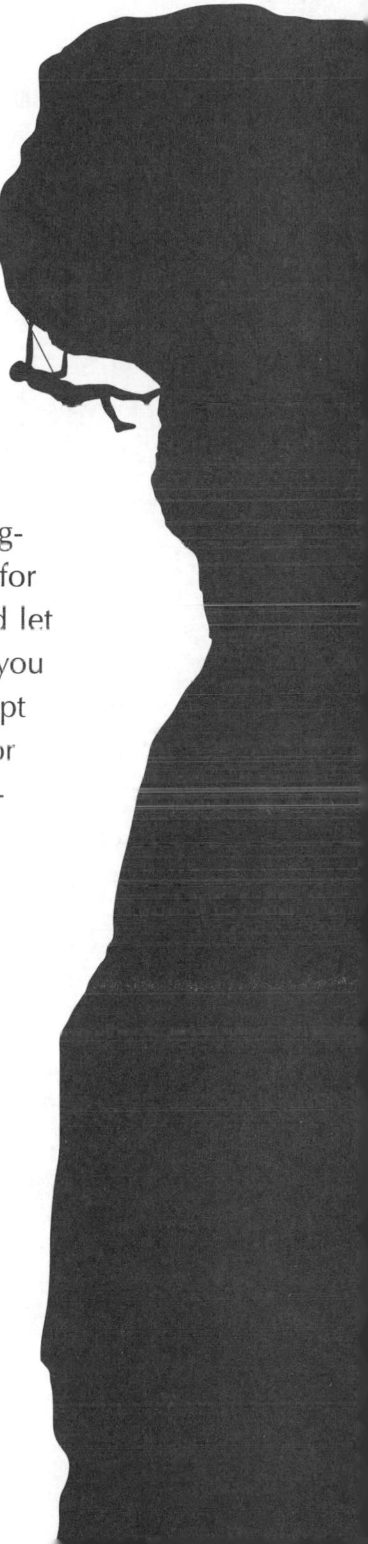

Dig into the Bible and find the verses that speak to your issues. If that's not doing it, then talk to people who know God's Word better than you do, like your pastor. Find out what they believe God could be wanting you to learn from your problems.

This might seem like a small thing, but spiritually speaking, it's huge. It's taking what the enemy would have you keep in the dark and bringing it out into the light where it can get all cleaned up. And it's the start of a new way of life. When you get good at looking at everything that happens to you as important for your spiritual growth, then nothing ever again can harm you—it may hurt emotionally or even physically, but it cannot harm you because you will trust the pain to the Lord, knowing that he will work it all out for good.

If you've taken this step, then congratulations, you've started to get over it! We're proud of you. This step is a big one on the road to redemption. Making something good out of what the world would tell you is bad is the gift of faith. The death of Jesus should have been a tragedy—a sad ending to a short but important life—but this tragedy is our salvation. And your tragedy can be someone else's hope if you are first

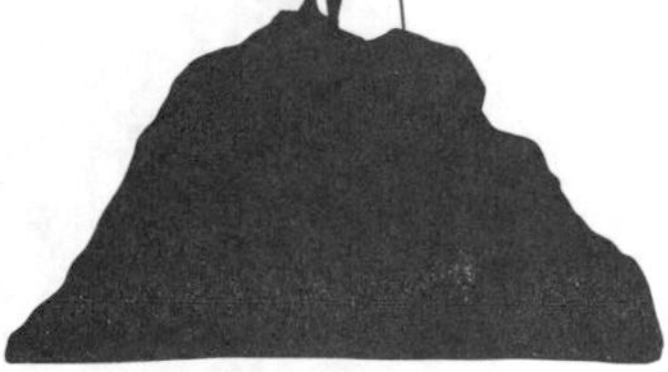

willing to wash it with God's Word. You will be set free at the point when you refuse to let sin continue to attack you, strangle you, or control you. Letting go and getting over it removes the chains of sin's control. Holding on and refusing to get over it keeps you in bondage.

> I waited patiently for the Lord.
> He turned to me and heard my cry for help.
> He pulled me out of a horrible pit,
> out of the mud and clay.
> He set my feet on a rock
> and made my steps secure. (Ps. 40:1–2)

Reconciliation

A lot of times the thing you need to get over involves someone else. They've done something bad, so you've broken off the relationship with them. This happens a lot because we are all human, we all mess up, and we all hurt each other, and without an understanding of God's call to forgive and get over it, it can be hard to keep relationships healthy and strong. But God is very concerned about good relationships. The Bible talks about reconciliation (or restoration, depending on what translation you are reading), and it means restoring a broken relationship.

Now, this doesn't necessarily mean getting back together with your ex, but it does mean giving some

"If you have been putting off going to another person to try to achieve reconciliation with him, you have wronged *him*."

Jay Adams, *Christian Living in the Home*

humble thought to where you might need to apologize and attempt to restore things with friends and family. Jesus says it this way: "So if you are offering your gift at the altar and remember there that another believer has something against you, leave your gift at the altar. First go away and make peace with that person. Then come back and offer your gift" (Matt. 5:23–24).

This description of what to do if someone has something against you doesn't give you any leeway to say, "But they started it" or "But I've got too much to do." It makes it clear that if someone has something against you or if your relationship is broken, then you've got to go make peace with them before you do anything else. Be aware, though, that they might not be on the same page as you. They might not be ready to work things out, they might not want anything to do with you, and you will have no control over that, but "as much as it is possible, live in peace with everyone" (Rom. 12:18). You can only do what you can do, and how they respond isn't on you, but you are to be someone bent on peace and doing what is holy in God's sight. The only thing you can control is what you do, and if God tells you to go fix things, then go fix things and leave others' reactions to them.

The amazing thing about all that God commands us to do is that he does it as well. He doesn't ask us to do things he is unwilling to do. In 2 Corinthians you can see what we mean:

> God has done all this. He has restored our relationship with him through Christ, and has given us this ministry of restoring relationships. In other words, God was using Christ to restore his relationship with humanity. He didn't hold people's faults against them, and he has given us this message of restored relationships to tell others. (2 Cor. 5:18–19)

How can we accept God's restoration of our relationship with him and not then go and do the same with others? If God doesn't hold people's faults against them, then why would we? Are we more holy than God, that we should judge people more harshly? The truth is that your standards can't be higher than God's, especially when his allow for reconciliation in the lives of the broken and sinful people in your life. God does it, and so should you.

Finally Over It

If you suffer with any kind of chronic emotional pain or have a recurring problem in your life, then now is the time to humbly choose to get over it. While telling someone to "get over it" might sound uncaring and harsh, we hope that by now you understand what we are getting at. If you can't get over something, then you are stuck behind it or under it. And that means it will forever be an obstacle to your life. Your purpose in this world can never be fulfilled as long as you hold on to sin and nurse it like a baby kitten. Coddling your pain and making excuses for why you feel the way you do does no one any good. It's like digging a hole under the huge boulder of your problem and saying, "I can't help it—this boulder just won't get off my back." How untrue. You can choose to be done with any emotional suffering by changing your focus: instead of sticking close to your boulder, you can crawl up on top of it and get a better view of the land. Make it your new vantage point and not the stone rolled over your grave.

One thing we want you to remember in all of this was said by John Ortberg in *The Me I Want to Be*: "God isn't at work producing the circumstances you want. God is at work in bad circumstances producing the you he wants." When you can know this beyond a shadow of a doubt, you can find joy in your suffering, as it says in James 1:2. Becoming a better person takes trials, it takes testing, and it takes pain—not pain you inflict on yourself but pain that comes from outside of you, pain that seems unfair and unjust

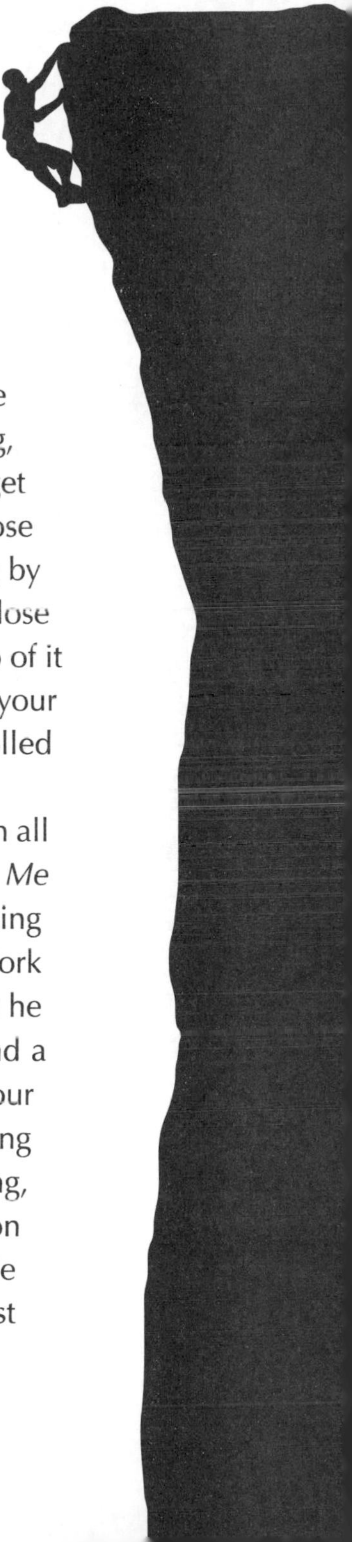

but that from heaven looks like the thing that makes you holy.

As Charles Spurgeon said in his sermon "Contentment,"

> Remember that all these sufferings are less than his sufferings. "Can't you watch with your Lord one hour?" He hangs upon the tree with a world's miseries in his bowels; can't you bear these lesser miseries that fall on you? Remember that all these chastenings work for your good; they are all making you ready; every stroke of your Father's rod is bringing you nearer to perfection.

Don't waste the strokes on feeling sorry for yourself or holding a grudge. Your sinful reaction to God's rod on your back gets you nowhere but further into the pain and suffering. Trust that God can and will use what you can get over for your benefit. And remember the words of Hebrews 12:7–11 when it comes to the hardship you must endure:

> Endure your discipline. God corrects you as a father corrects his children. All children are disciplined by their fathers. If you aren't disciplined like the other children, you aren't part of the family. On earth we have fathers who disciplined us, and we respect them. Shouldn't we place ourselves under the authority of God, the father of spirits, so that we will live? For a short time our fathers disciplined us as they thought best. Yet, God disciplines us for our own good so that we can become holy like him. We don't enjoy being disciplined. It always seems to cause more pain than joy. But later on, those who learn from that discipline have peace that comes from doing what is right.

When you trust the Father, you can trust the pain to lead you to him. Don't let it be wasted. Don't let it divert your gaze or take your attention, but allow it to teach you more about the One who loves you and to make you more like him. You know the saying that what doesn't destroy you will make you stronger. When it comes to the things of the past, you have two choices: let them destroy you or let them make you stronger. No one else can choose for you. Today is the day—will you set your past free or hold on for dear life? We hope you choose freedom. And for this we pray,

Father, set me free from the pains of my past. Teach me to get over what needs to be gotten over and to get on with you. Thank you for the gift of your Son and the freedom he brings. To you I give all my wounds, pain, and suffering, and I trust you to use it for good. Thank you for knowing just what to do and for willingly doing it. I love you. Amen.

Hayley DiMarco is founder of Hungry Planet, where she writes and creates cutting-edge books that connect with the multitasking mind-set. She has written and co-written numerous bestselling books for both teens and adults, including *Dateable, Mean Girls, Sexy Girls, Technical Virgin, B4UD8,* and *God Girl.*

Michael DiMarco is the publisher and creative director of Hungry Planet. He has written and co-written numerous bestselling books for both teens and adults, including *God Guy, Cupidity, B4UD8, Unstuff, All In,* and *Almost Sex.*

Michael and Hayley live with their daughter in Nashville, Tennessee.

At godgirl.com, you can be mentored by bestselling author Hayley DiMarco in what it means to be a God Girl and get help with the challenges of life in the process.

Here are just some of the features of godgirl.com:

- Free books, resources, and an online Bible to grow in your relationship with God.
- God Girl Academy is a four-part spiritual mentoring course you can go through on your own or as part of a group.
- Quick Relief section gives you Bible verses organized by the topics you need at the moment.
- Exclusive live online events with Hayley and her friends.
- Design Your Own GG Bible cover hints and templates for the one and only all-white blank canvas God Girl Bible.
- And much, much more!

And if you're a leader of a small group, you can use godgirl.com as a meeting hub and resource library full of tools for discipleship and mentoring young women.

<iFuse> beta

life + faith + love + truth

Chat with Hayley and connect with friends on Hungry Planet's new online social community, iFuse.com.

Main | Invite | My Page | Members | Groups | Forum

Page | Friends | Blog

Hayley DiMarco's Page

Latest Activity

Hayley DiMarco left a comment for Brittany
1 day ago

Erin left a comment for Hayley DiMarco
1 day ago

Taylor and Hayley DiMarco are now friends

1 day ago

Hayley DiMarco added the blog post 'Sexy Fashion Fixes'
1 day ago

Hayley DiMarco left a comment for Erin
1 day ago

Hayley DiMarco left a comment for Katie
1 day ago

Hayley DiMarco
Female
Nashville, TN, United States
+ Add as friend
Send a Message
Share

Hayley DiMarco is chief creative officer and founder of Hungry Planet, where she writes and creates cutting-edge books that connect with the multitasking mind-set. She has written and co-written numerous bestselling books for both teens and adults, including *Dateable*, *Mean Girls*, *Sexy Girls*, and *Technical Virgin*. She and her husband, Michael, live in Nashville, Tennessee.

Revell
a division of Baker Publishing Group
www.RevellBooks.com

Hungry Planet
www.hungryplanet.net

<iFuse> beta
life + faith + love + truth